80-10-10

Everyman's Road to Riches

Dr. Gene Lingerfelt

80-10-10

ISBN: 978-0-9824145-4-5

Published by

LIFEBRIDGE
BOOKS
P.O. BOX 49428
CHARLOTTE, NC 28277

Printed in the United States of America.

Contents

INTRODUCTION

If you are content to live a mediocre, average life, struggling with finances and "barely making it," don't waste your time reading this book. Give it to someone else!

But if you believe, as I do, that God wants you to abundantly prosper, what you are about to learn will transform your financial future.

This is not some "pie in the sky" theory based on wishful thinking. How do I know? Because this 80-10-10 lifestyle has produced a harvest in my life that is far greater than I could have ever imagined. And now I want to share it with you.

You are about to discover an action plan and a development strategy that will dramatically increase your wealth factor and cause you to become financially independent over time. If faithfully followed, it will work for anybody!

PROVEN PRINCIPLES

From reading and studying scripture, I believe it is God's will for us to prosper in everything we put our hands to. Our heavenly Father gives us the "ability" to produce wealth, but it is only when we take action that He responds by adding His favor and blessing.

If you think you are helpless, this will be your fate. But I want to give you specific keys to prospering and pulling ahead based on bedrock, proven principles. If you use them, the wealth of God's world is yours.

We will discuss His divine plan regarding the money that flows through your hands—what portion belongs to you and what is God's. For example, you will learn that the covenant of tithing was not instituted to take money *from* you. Just the opposite; it is God's way of giving abundance *to* you.

A DRAMATIC CHANGE

Many of the wealthiest people on our planet started with practically nothing, but made a personal commitment to invest and save a specific portion of every dollar they received.

Regardless of your present circumstances, be encouraged. I want to show you how you can make simple adjustments in your daily habits that will dramatically change your financial situation. I firmly believe that becoming a millionaire in America should be the norm rather than the exception.

Finally, you will learn how to apply the principles of

sowing and reaping—to produce a harvest that is "above and beyond" what you need or expect.

I have proven that by continually giving, saving, investing, and sowing, my supply increases. And the more I give, the more God expands my "store" of seed.

Today I am praying that you will step out in faith and start walking on God's road of abundance. It begins with the work of your hands—to produce the initial financial resources you need for this exciting journey.

After reading this book, if you will make an unbreakable covenant with God to live the 80-10-10 life, I guarantee you will receive blessing, abundance, and the favor He has promised.

Let's get started.

– Dr. Gene Lingerfelt

One

The Power of Industry and Diligence

The miracle, or the power, that elevates the few is to be found in their industry, application, and perseverance under the prompting of a brave, determined spirit.

–Mark Twain

What you are about to discover is a simple, yet profound strategy for a lifetime of personal fulfillment and financial success.

Perhaps you looked at the title of this book and wondered, "Eighty-10-10—what could this possibly mean?"

As you will learn, it is a formula as to how you handle the money that flows through your hands.

Breaking it down into dollars and cents, out of every dollar, 80 cents is yours to keep and spend as you choose. However, what you do with the two "ten cent" pieces determines how you will prosper both spiritually and materially. We will discuss this in later chapters.

THE FIRST STEP

There is a common misunderstanding among many Christians. They attempt to use faith in God as a solution to problems that can only be solved through planning and action.

For example, let's talk about being overweight. I've met sincere believers who ask the Lord to take their excess pounds off, when all that is really needed is an action plan, will-power, determination, and consistency.

The same principle applies to both work and investments. Speaking personally, I don't sit at home, laze around, do nothing, and then expect God to bless me. This is foolish, because if you take zero and multiply it by a thousand, you still get zero.

So we have to start with *something*—and that something is the result of our industry and work. In other words, we must *earn* money to *have* money. Without this first step, there is nothing to give or grow.

To increase your wealth factor and become financially independent over time, you need an action plan and a development strategy that is faithfully followed. It will work for anybody.

I am using the word "industry" instead of "labor" because industry is defined as self-generated or self-motivated labor. This is work that doesn't have to be supervised. Industry is also listed as one of Benjamin Franklin's "Thirteen Virtues."

Franklin counseled, "Sloth makes all things difficult, but industry, all things easy. He that rises late must trot all day, and shall scarce overtake his business at night, while laziness travels so slowly that poverty soon overtakes him."

SOMETHING FOR NOTHING?

There is a spirit prevalent in our nation that I refer to as a "spirit of free lunch." Remember, something without a price attached to it is rarely worth having.

> ***There is a spirit prevalent in our nation that I refer to as a "spirit of free lunch."***

We see this everywhere. A man desires a loving wife—but he doesn't want to be a faithful husband. An employee expects a fair day's wage—but doesn't put in a full day's work.

Many approach the Almighty with the same attitude. They want something for nothing, thinking God is Santa Claus or the Easter bunny.

God's rewards, however, are based on an entirely different premise. The Bible states this principle: "Without faith it is impossible to please God, because anyone who comes to him must believe that he exists and that he rewards those who earnestly seek him" (Hebrews 11:6).

RULES FOR REWARDS

Over the years I have had people tell me, "I'm just not into that faith stuff."

My answer has always been the same. "Well, I'm sorry to hear you're not into pleasing God, because the Bible teaches that without faith it is impossible to please Him."

Scripture doesn't state that without faith it is *difficult* to please Him; it is *impossible!*

Earlier in my life, when I finally awakened to the fact that God is a rewarder, my entire outlook changed. And yours will too. By fully obeying the Lord, you can expect amazing things to happen.

When people join a health club and sign on the

dotted line, there are rules and requirements they agree to follow. Yet, many are of the opinion that they can reach heaven without knowing the rules God requires for entry. Yes, there is a price to pay, but in comparison to the rewards, the cost is insignificant.

WHERE IS THE POWER?

Look closely at the words of the apostle Paul: "Now to him who is able to do immeasurably more than all we ask or imagine, according to his power that is at work within us, to him be glory" (Ephesians 3:20-21).

Where is the power at work? "Within us"—in you and me.

Most Christians think if they could only produce more faith they would receive a miracle and all their troubles would be over. But whatever God is going to do *in* your life, He is going to do *through* your life. So you'd better join the real world and demonstrate some industry and diligence!

> ***Whatever God is going to do in your life, He is going to do through your life.***

There is tremendous practical insight and wisdom written in the Word of God and we must implement its teachings.

As a pastor, I see far too many people *trying* the Word of God, yet not enough *doing* the Word.

"NO STONE UNTURNED"

I continually meet men and women who are desperately searching for a financial miracle. But I have discovered that prosperity results from a combination of utilizing and demonstrating the practical wisdom of the Word, plus standing in faith that the Lord will give you the desires of your heart. It's what I call "leaving no stone unturned."

My wife and I learned long ago that if there were not enough resources in our home we had to take action—and it always involved work. When we performed our part, God did His, and we were blessed.

When we performed our part, God did His, and we were blessed.

Let's take a look at Isaac, the son of Abraham. The Bible tells us that in a time of terrible famine when Isaac was tempted to go down to Egypt in search of provision, God told him: "Stay in this land for a while, and I will be with you and will bless you" (Genesis 26:3).

What was Isaac's response? As impossible as it may seem, in that dry parched earth he did something in the natural: "Isaac planted crops in that land and the same year reaped a hundredfold" (verse 12).

How could this happen? "Because the Lord blessed him" (verse 12).

The supernatural was taking place. Even though God told Isaac a blessing was about to occur, he didn't sit around waiting for a UPS or FedEx delivery to arrive. Isaac immediately went to work and planted seed.

However, the principle I want you to grasp is that it is not simply human effort alone that produces great results. Nor is it only by faith that we prosper. Rather, when our work is combined with God's blessing, the sky's the limit. In Isaac's case, we read how he "became rich, and his wealth continued to grow" (Genesis 26:13).

Are You Doing Your Part?

Even though I live by spiritual principles and practice the laws of faith, God has never dropped by my house and mowed the lawn or trimmed my hedges. Neither has He taken the bills out of my mailbox and written out the checks.

You see, God will not do for me what I can do for myself. For example, I shouldn't need His help with my diet. As an educated adult I should know the difference between what is good for my body and what isn't. The Lord doesn't wake me up in the middle of the night, put me on a leash, and walk me through the neighborhood like a puppy so I can get my exercise. He expects me to have enough common sense to take care of my body.

Yet there may come a time when we've done all we can and have reached our human limit. Perhaps our body needs to be healed. This is where God steps in.

I've been asked, "What if we fail to do what we can. Will the Lord bless us anyhow?"

No, because He would be contributing to our delinquency. To me, this is no different than what the government does by handing out welfare checks to healthy individuals who are fully capable of holding down a job and yet refuse to work for their own living.

A Pattern for Increase

From reading and studying scripture, I believe it is God's will for us to prosper in everything we put our hands to. And this is the key. When we take action, God responds by adding His favor and blessing.

When we take action, God responds by adding His favor and blessing.

The first thing on God's agenda after creating Adam and Eve in the Garden of Eden was to bless them. Instead of threatening or instilling fear, the Lord said, "Be fruitful and increase in number; fill the earth and subdue it" (Genesis 1:28).

I am constantly amazed at how many people have tried to turn financial prosperity into a doctrine of the devil and success into an evil of Satan. Right from the very beginning of time, God set a pattern for "increase."

POOR NO MORE!

As we previously mentioned, God bragged about the abundance of Isaac. He was also proud of Abraham, who "had become very wealthy in livestock and in silver and gold" (Genesis 13:1).

If being financially successful is not part of God's divine plan for His children, we would not be told, "Beloved, I wish above all things that thou mayest prosper and be in health, even as thy soul prospereth" (3 John 2 KJV). This is the will of God.

The Lord said to the children of Israel, "There should be no poor among you, for in the land the Lord your God is giving you to possess as your inheritance, he will richly bless you" (Deuteronomy 15:4).

But there is a condition to the promise: "...if only you fully obey the Lord your God and are careful to follow all these commands I am giving you today. For the Lord your God will bless you as he has promised, and you will lend to many nations but will borrow from none. You will rule over many nations but none will rule over you" (verses 5-6).

If this was true of the "servants of the Most High" referred to in the Old Testament (Daniel 3:26), how much more should it apply to New Testament believers who are called the "sons of God" (Galatians 3:26)?

BUILD YOUR BASE

How can God honor and bless the work of your hands if they are idle? The path to prosperity starts with being industrious enough to find a job—and diligent enough to keep it.

How can God honor and bless the work of your hands if they are idle?

There are those who complain, "I've been searching for work, but can't find exactly what I am looking for."

What a lame excuse! You may wind up in the lousiest place of employment in the world. Do not be discouraged. You are only there for a season, earning wages and building your base. Faithfully apply yourself to whatever task you are assigned.

In the words of General George Patton, "Always do more than is required of you."

Just as cream rises to the top, you will be promoted. So never give up!

TWO

THE SIX KEYS TO PROSPERING AND PULLING AHEAD

Success usually comes to those who are too busy to be looking for it.

– HENRY DAVID THOREAU

I once told an audience, "Here's all I need to know to predict your future. Show me your front yard—show me your car—and show me your shoes."

My remark came as a shock to some, but I was absolutely serious. If your car is clean and polished and your shoes are shined, I can see instantly that you have bright days ahead. But if I drive by your house and there are overgrown shrubs and paint peeling off your gutters, chances are slim that you will be successful. The die has been cast.

You shouldn't drive to work with hubcaps missing

from your car, or looking like you just tumbled out of a clothing donation center.

I was encouraging people to take pride in their appearance—and to be the very best at what they do. As scripture asks, "Do you see a man skilled in his work? He will serve before kings; he will not serve before obscure men" (Proverbs 22:29).

In this chapter I want to share six keys that will make your tomorrow far better than today.

KEY #1

IF YOU WANT TO PROSPER AND PULL AHEAD:

YOU HAVE TO DO SOMETHING ABOUT YOUR DREAM

The ability to dream and imagine sets us apart and makes us different than the rest of creation.

In the beginning, the earth was formless and empty. Then God began to imagine all that He was about to create—the sun and moon, trees and flowers, animals and birds. Next, He spoke what He envisioned into existence.

When it came to man, however, He placed within us the same dominion, authority, and creativity He possesses. We each have these gifts because we are made in His image (See Genesis 1:26-27). And, like our Creator, we have an eternal soul and spirit.

Animals do things instinctively. You never see a bird build a nest one way this year, and another way the next. Animals do what they are genetically programmed to do, while you and I are unique. We have been given the ability to dream and see our visions become reality.

Animals do what they are genetically programmed to do, while you and I are unique.

The problem, however, is that many misuse this gift. In fact, one of Satan's strategies is to cause you to waste and squander your thoughts and imagination.

A Time for Action

Thankfully, the Lord doesn't ask us to have identical dreams.

I have two children, a son and a daughter—and they each have different visions for their future. This is perfectly fine with God, as long as their dreams are consistent with the Word.

The benefit of desiring some particular object is that it inspires you to get off your couch and go for it. In other words, you have to act on your dream. As scripture tells us, "Lazy hands make a man poor, but diligent hands bring wealth. He who gathers crops in summer is a wise son, but he who sleeps during harvest is a disgraceful son" (Proverbs 10:4-5).

> ***Abundance comes naturally to those who are willing to do whatever is required.***

Abundance comes naturally to those who are willing to do whatever is required. "A sluggard does not plow in season; so at harvest time he looks but finds nothing" (Proverbs 20:4).

If you toil all week and receive your paycheck on Friday and your co-worker "sluffs off" and gets fired, don't shed any tears for him. You both receive what you deserve.

The Bible bluntly tells us, "If a man will not work, he shall not eat" (2 Thessalonians 3:10).

If the governors of some states would make this a law, they would cut welfare payments by ninety percent and help balance their budgets!

There is a time for dreaming and a time for action. Remember, "All hard work brings a profit, but mere talk leads only to poverty" (Proverbs 14:23).

Each and every one of us can do whatever we set our minds to.

KEY #2

IF YOU WANT TO PROSPER AND PULL AHEAD:

YOU MUST GIVE GOD SOMETHING TO BLESS

One day Jesus was teaching on a hillside and there were five thousand people present listening to His every word. Late in the afternoon, His disciples suggested that He send the crowd away to the nearby villages so they could find food and lodging. However, Jesus told the disciples to give the people something to eat.

Philip answered Him, "Eight months' wages would not buy enough bread for each one to have a bite!" (John 6:7).

Then Andrew spoke up and said, "Here is a boy with five small barley loaves and two small fish, but how far will they go among so many?" (verse 8).

But this seeming dilemma was no challenge for Jesus. He asked the crowd to sit down, then He blessed the loaves and fishes and the disciples started feeding the hungry throng.

It was a miracle! Scripture records, "When they had all had enough to eat, he said to his disciples, 'Gather the pieces that are left over. Let nothing be wasted'" (verse 12).

There were twelve baskets full of leftovers (verse 13).

There was more than enough to satisfy the five thousand. But what initiated the entire process was the fact that the Lord was given something to bless.

LITTLE BY LITTLE

Yes, there are times when the supernatural takes place, but in most cases you start with what you have and make it multiply—regardless of how long it takes.

As Solomon wrote, "Dishonest money dwindles away, but he who gathers money little by little makes it grow" (Proverbs 13:11).

This means giving God what He can bless on a regular, consistent basis.

Never forget the source of your abundance.

Never forget the source of your abundance. As Moses told the people long ago, "You may say to yourself, 'My power and the strength of my hands have produced this wealth for me.' But remember the Lord your God, for it is he who gives you the ability to produce wealth" (Deuteronomy 8:17-18).

The King James version says it this way: "...it is He who gives you power to get wealth."

This brings us to the question: If God gives you the capability to produce riches, how can wealth be bad?

How can it be wrong for you to have enough money to buy your children clothes for school or build up enough resources to send them to a university?

According to the Word, abundance is not evil.

The Right Stuff!

One man told me, "Pastor, I'm trying the Word."

I answered him, "No, the Word is trying you—to see if you are made of the right stuff!"

It's amazing to me that so many give Satan far more time to work in their lives than they give God. It is no wonder they are trapped and entangled in the world.

The Lord blesses us in many ways, including rewarding a spirit of generosity. "Give generously to him and do so without a grudging heart; then because of this the Lord your God will bless you in all your work and in everything you put your hand to" (Deuteronomy 15:10).

Since this is true, it is obvious that the way to have an increase is to start more projects and assume more responsibility.

In the process you have to take care of business.

Today, because of the environment we are in, there are legal implications to everything—and each year it becomes more intensive. So just because you start new ventures doesn't mean you can walk off and leave behind what you have already begun.

A LIFE-CHANGING DECISION

There are times when just one choice can make a tremendous difference.

I remember the inflationary days of the Jimmy Carter presidency. My father-in-law had saved a substantial amount for his retirement and the City of Cincinnati, Ohio, was offering 20-year bonds to finance Riverfront Stadium at a guaranteed 14.75% annual interest rate.

He invested the entire amount—which proved to be the greatest financial decision of his lifetime.

A DIVINE CONNECTION

As a believer, you have a distinct advantage. In your daily prayer life the Holy Spirit can speak to you regarding any decision—whether it concerns your family, your career, or your finances.

There have been moments in my fellowship with the Lord when He has given me clear direction concerning decisions I needed to make. Some involved personnel working in our ministry, and others had to do with handling finances.

Once you have committed your life to the Lord you have a spiritual connection to your heavenly Father. But if you never take advantage of this relationship, what's the point of being connected?

Since there are benefits available from heaven, exercise your divine right to access what is rightfully yours. Don't hesitate to ask the Lord to tell you what is on the horizon. You will sense His leading.

Don't hesitate to ask the Lord to tell you what is on the horizon.

If your company offers you a transfer, take out a calculator and figure out the finances. At the same time, get on your knees and talk to God concerning your future. The Holy Spirit knows whether this move is right for you and your family, so listen to His voice. Why operate on a hit-and-miss basis when you can go for guidance to the One who loves you the most?

He will always lead you to green pastures, never into a muddy ditch.

Give the Lord something to bless—your faith and

your finances, because nothing is too small for God. But know that what you present to Him will not remain small. It will grow and prosper beyond all you can ask or think. He is the God of multiplication!

KEY #3
IF YOU WANT TO PROSPER AND PULL AHEAD:
YOU MUST PROVE YOURSELF TRUSTWORTHY

Can you be trusted with someone else's property?

I surround myself with individuals I feel I could hand a suitcase containing $1 million and tell them I want it back in thirty days—and not lose a moment's sleep.

> ***How can you believe God for great things when you are not trustworthy with what you already have?***

What about you? Should others have the confidence to place their faith in your character and behavior? Are you stealing office supplies and taking them home? Are you fudging your expense account? I hope not.

How can you believe God for great things when you are not trustworthy with what you already have?

Jesus spoke directly to this issue when He said, "Whoever can be trusted with very little can also be trusted with much, and whoever is dishonest with very little will also be dishonest with much. So if you have not been trustworthy in handling worldly wealth, who will trust you with true riches? And if you have not been trustworthy with someone else's property, who will give you property of your own?" (Luke 16:10-12).

The typical Christian offers the excuse, "When I make $50,000 I'll start giving to God's work."

They have their priorities backwards. Jesus said whoever can be trusted with little can be trusted with much.

Promises You Can Depend On

It is certainly not wrong to pray for riches in the here and now. Look closely at the Lord's Prayer—the model we are to follow: "Our Father in heaven, hallowed be your name, your kingdom come, your will be done on earth as it is in heaven" (Matthew 6:9-10).

Are there dirt roads in heaven? No, the streets are paved with gold. And will we be living in mobile homes? No, Jesus promised, "In my Father's house are many mansions: if it were not so, I would have told you. I go to prepare a place for you. And if I go and prepare a place for you, I will come again, and receive you unto myself; that where I am, there ye may be also" (John 14:2-3).

It is God's will for us to live in abundance here on earth—just as we will experience in the celestial city.

You can trust His Word.

KEY #4

IF YOU WANT TO PROSPER AND PULL AHEAD:

BE A WEALTH PRODUCER

The industrious create their own opportunities. It is amazing how doors will swing open the more you apply yourself.

Everyone has at least one relative who knows how to criticize your way of life, commenting negatively on how you raise your family, even passing an opinion on the clothes you wear. Sadly, this same person rarely contributes anything positive or encouraging.

I've learned that the best way to handle such individuals is to ignore them. If somebody is always tearing you down, why pay them any attention?

Also ignore "ankle biters." These are the bottom-feeders and slackards who are "moochers," not producers.

I've observed men and women who attend church purely to sell each other insurance, cruises, investments

—anything with a dollar attached. This may keep money in circulation, but the church is not the place to do business.

What is needed are real producers. If this means pumping gas—be the best gas-pumper in the city you live in. And before long you may be managing the station, and some day own it.

A Testimony of Productivity

Why waste your God-given skills by doing a job halfway when you can do it the *right* way?

> ***Why waste your God-given skills by doing a job halfway when you can do it the right way?***

As followers of Christ we should be examples to the world of what it means to be productive. It's not surprising that some business owners have no time for Christians because their experience has been less than stellar. As one man commented, "I hired a woman who constantly tried to convert her associates, injected Jesus into every conversation, and spent her break time reading the Bible. No one wanted to be around her and she was the worst employee I've ever had."

Your testimony will be judged by your productivity.

"GIG" THAT FROG!

When I was a boy, there were some lowlands on the property where my father's mother lived—and you could always find frogs down there. My friends and I loved to mess around with those creatures.

Here's what I learned. You can hardly get a frog to move unless you "gig" it. To us, that meant touching the frog in the rear end with a stick.

> ***If you need a task-master to get going, you'd better have a heart-to-heart talk with yourself.***

Those days often spring to mind, especially when a person comes to work on a project at our house and is bone lazy. I wonder how they ever make a living. I'm often tempted to gig them into productivity!

If you are hardwired to be shiftless, you'll have great difficulty being a success. And if you need a task-master to get going, you'd better have a heart-to-heart talk with yourself.

Why should anyone have to order you, "Do the job properly—and get it done on time"?

Make the decision to be a self-starter and remind yourself of it every day until productivity becomes a habit.

Iron Sharpens Iron

Be careful of your relationships. It's a major problem when good people become connected to the wrong person—whether it be a friend, a business partner, or a pastor.

Chose your associates wisely— and spend the vast majority of your time with those who are already a success. They will lift you up instead of dragging you down.

If you plan to be a producer, hang out with producers! As the Bible says, "As iron sharpens iron, so one man sharpens another" (Proverbs 27:17).

"Whatever I Do Prospers!"

The wisdom and instruction you glean from the writers of scripture will give you a head start on the road to abundance.

"Blessed is the man who does not walk in the counsel of the wicked or stand in the way of sinners or sit in the seat of mockers. But his delight is in the law of the Lord, and on his law he meditates day and night. He is like a tree planted by streams of water, which yields its fruit in season and whose leaf does not wither. Whatever he does prospers" (Psalm 1:1-3).

Read those last four words again. If you turn your back on sin and spend quality time in the Word, you will start producing and every action of your life will be prosperous.

No one in Old Testament days knew more about success than David. His words were written from a place of experience.

Follow his example and speak with confidence and expectation about your present and your future. Stand up and declare, "Whatever I do prospers!"

Today, start being proactive instead of reactive.

Is Money Evil?

Money is neutral; it is neither bad nor good. It all depends on the person who has ownership. If you place $1 million in the hand of Osama bin Laden, something evil is going to happen. But if that same amount is given to the work of God, I can guarantee wonderful results.

Knowing this, make it your objective to see that every possible resource is removed from the enemy's camp and transferred to God's Kingdom.

Golden Nuggets

Instead of producing wealth, far too many are wasting time, waiting for the answer to suddenly appear out of the blue. If you are sitting around expecting someone else to pay your light bill, you may soon be living in the dark.

What a nerve-wracking way to exist!

If you are sitting around expecting someone else to pay your light bill, you may soon be living in the dark.

God gives you the ability to produce and the power to generate wealth. You don't walk down a path, stumble over a rock and suddenly find $1,000. No one has ever walked out of their home in the morning and found that the dew on the grass has turned into golden nuggets.

Instead, apply the principles of God's Word and start producing. When you do, the Lord will find a way to bring increase. One gentleman told me, "My company couldn't find a way to give me a raise in my present job, so they offered me a promotion!"

When the Almighty is in charge there is no telling what will transpire. In scripture we are told, "The king's heart is in the hand of the Lord; he directs it like a watercourse wherever he pleases" (Proverbs 21:1).

Our source is not our boss, the government, or Wall Street—it is God. And He will give you the power to produce wealth.

KEY #5

IF YOU WANT TO PROSPER AND PULL AHEAD

DETERMINE TO BE SELF-MOTIVATED

I was sitting on my patio last fall watching a lone squirrel. My, was he busy! Totally energized and motivated, he scampered around the oak trees, picked up acorns, and took them to a safe place to store for the winter.

I thought, "He doesn't have a foreman or a Harvard MBA telling him what to do." Yet he is diligent in going about his business.

This reminded me of the advice of Solomon when he wrote: "Go to the ant, you sluggard; consider its ways and be wise! It has no commander, no overseer or ruler, yet it stores its provisions in summer and gathers its food at harvest. How long will you lie there, you sluggard? When will you get up from your sleep? A little sleep, a little slumber, a little folding of the hands to rest—and poverty will come on you like a bandit and scarcity like an armed man" (Proverbs 6:6-11).

In today's politically correct world, there are those who would say that a sluggard is just a person who is emotionally challenged, but the Word tells it like it is. And as I told my congregation, "Sometimes it will just jerk the slack right out of you!"

Step Up to the Plate

Don't fall into the trap of believing everything the media is telling you. They present their opinion as though it were absolute fact.

I recently saw a public school educator speaking on television about the need for sex education in the classroom as though he had just descended from Mount Sinai. When you listen to the judgments of others, stop and ask yourself, "Is this really the way it is?"

If you've made a mistake and things have gone wrong, shake it off, pick yourself up, and start over again.

Today, you may feel pressure from those who don't want you to forge ahead, because it makes them feel uncomfortable.

If you've made a mistake and things have gone wrong, shake it off, pick yourself up and start over again. If you are waiting for someone to come along and encourage you—it may be a long wait!

Why get so discouraged that you stop applying yourself and give up? You may be up to bat when Satan throws one negative pitch and you will stop swinging. But you will never hit a home run until you step up to the plate and try again.

> ***Dust yourself off and get back in the game!***

Encourage yourself in the Lord, dust yourself off and get back in the game!

Key #6

If You Want to Prosper and Pull Ahead:

Remember, It Is the Diligent Who See Their Dreams Come to Pass

Africa is the richest continent on the planet. Hidden beneath the earth are gold, diamonds, and valuable minerals beyond our imagination. And I can tell you from first-hand experience that its people are some of the friendliest and most genuine I have ever met.

With all this potential, why is the continent so

impoverished? It is because of corrupt government officials who rape the riches of the land to accumulate their own fortunes. They have destroyed dreams and made personal diligence of no value.

Think about the Republic of Zimbabwe. At one time it flourished as the nation of Southern Rhodesia. But today, under the heavy-handed rule of Robert Mugabe, the country is in shambles. Violence and runaway inflation have made life unbearable.

With many leaders who steal everything they can get their hands on, the future of Africa remains bleak. On that continent, potential and realization are two totally different things.

Thank God, you and I live in an environment where persistence still pays dividends.

The Results of Diligence

The wealthiest man who ever lived, King Solomon, knew the value of being diligent. His wisdom and instructions are timeless:

- "Diligent hands will rule, but laziness ends in slave labor" (Proverbs 12:24).

- "The lazy man does not roast his game, but the diligent man prizes his possessions" (Proverbs 12:27).

- "The sluggard craves and gets nothing, but the desires of the diligent are fully satisfied" (Proverbs 13:4).

- "One who is slack in his work is brother to one who destroys" (Proverbs 18:9).

- "The plans of the diligent lead to profit as surely as haste leads to poverty" (Proverbs 21:5).

If you believe you are helpless, this will be your fate. But if there is just one small spark within you that whispers, "I can," the future is yours.

I pray you will apply these six keys—and that you will not just pull ahead but, with God's help, abundantly prosper.

THREE

THE BIG "TEN"

As a tither you automatically become solution-oriented rather than problem-oriented.

– MARK VICTOR HANSEN

If eighty percent of the money that we acquire through work, investments, inheritance, or from any other source is to spend as we please, what about the remainder?

It may come as a surprise to you, but ten percent of the money is not yours to begin with. It rightfully belongs to God, and you are only holding it temporarily until you can return it to Him.

We're talking about the tithe—God's admission price to His covenant of prosperity.

The word "tithe" as a noun means a tenth, or ten percent. But tithe is also a verb. When you bring your tithe to the storehouse there is action involved. And, as we will see, it unleashes an awesome power.

Let's begin with the basics. The ground you walk on doesn't belong to you. "The earth is the Lord's, and everything in it" (Psalm 24:1).

The ground you walk on doesn't belong to you.

Whether you are a farmer who grows crops, a miner who digs coal, or a carpenter who builds houses, you are using resources that were placed here by the Creator—and He still owns every inch of the land and the waters of the sea.

Since He has granted you the right to use His property, there is only one command He asks in return: "A tithe of everything from the land, whether grain from the soil or fruit from the trees, belongs to the Lord; it is holy to the Lord" (Leviticus 27:30).

YOUR CONNECTION

You say, "I don't believe in tithing. Ten percent is too high a percentage."

If this is your position, then you must generate the finances you can with your own strength and intelligence, but don't covet or get upset when others are supernaturally blessed by God.

The Lord is not going to cut the admission fee into His covenant of prosperity to five percent just because you choose not to believe in tithing.

Giving back to God what is His connects us to the Almighty and proves we are in agreement with His Word. It is what makes us compatible with our Holy God.

A covenant is actually a contract, but it's not a one-way agreement. It has to be advantageous for both parties.

He Brought "A Tenth"

When God made a covenant with Abraham, there were certain things He asked him to do. For example, the Lord said, "Leave your country, your people and your father's household and go to the land I will show you" (Genesis 12: 1).

If Abraham obeyed, here is what God promised in return, "I will make you into a great nation and I will bless you; I will make your name great...and all peoples on earth will be blessed through you" (verses 2-3).

There is another reason God richly poured out His favor on Abraham (called Abram before God changed his name). It involved the covenant of tithing.

After Abram returned from a victorious battle, "Then Melchizedek king of Salem brought out bread and wine. He was priest of God Most High, and he blessed Abram, saying, 'Blessed be Abram by God Most High, Creator of heaven and earth. And blessed be God Most High, who delivered your enemies into your hand.' Then Abram gave him a tenth of everything" (Genesis 14:18-20).

The tithe is a tangible demonstration that we are in covenant with God—even to this day. Remember, "If you belong to Christ, then you are Abraham's seed, and heirs according to the promise" (Galatians 3:29).

Just as Abraham presented his tenth to the High Priest, we give our tithe to the Lord. The Bible tells us that Jesus is the High Priest forever—"in the order of Melchizedek" (Hebrews 6:20).

BEYOND BELIEF

Millions profess to believe the Bible, yet they fail to practice its principles. They avoid obeying God's commands.

Belief is necessary, but more is required. For example, when you walk out of a shopping mall and climb into your car, you don't sit in the driver's seat and say, "I believe this car will start. I believe it will take me home."

You could sweet-talk your car all day and nothing would happen. Instead, you have to activate your belief by turning the key in the ignition and starting the engine.

Believing has its place, and we can find it in both saint and sinner. As James wrote,"You believe that there is one God. Good! Even the demons believe that—and shudder"(James 2:19)

I wish I could tell you that belief is all you need to experience everything God has for your life.

What benefit is that to the devil?

I wish I could tell you that belief is all you need to experience everything God has for your life. I've heard people say, "I believe the Word of God"—yet they are broke, sick, and defeated.

You can read the Bible from the Table of Contents to the Concordance, but you won't realize its marvelous truth until you act on its principles.

"DO" SOMETHING

If you study the miracles in the Bible, you will notice they are almost always preceded by some kind of action:

- Blind Bartimaeus called out to Jesus before he was healed (Mark 10:46-52).

- To a man who had been an invalid for thirty-eight years, Jesus said, "Pick up your mat and walk" and he was healed (John 5:8).

- The woman who had been bleeding for twelve years touched the hem of His garment and was made whole (Mark 5:25-34).

Action is also involved when we present our tithe. Because of our obedience, God promises that He will pour out such a blessing that we can hardly contain it (Malachi 3:10).

A PRICELESS GIFT

Salvation is free gift of God, yet He has instituted tithing as a requirement for His people. It never ceases to amaze me that average Christians think they are going to be blessed, healed, and go to heaven for less money than it costs to go to Disney World.

How can a person be in covenant with God when they drop $5 in the offering plate then go to their favorite restaurant for Sunday dinner and tip the waitress $7? She served you and your loved ones meat and potatoes, but God offers the priceless gift of salvation—yet you want to give her more!

We need to reexamine our thinking.

Blessings and Cursings

The tithe is called the "firstfruit"—which means you present a tenth of *all*—not after you have taken out your IRS deductions or subtracted your expenses.

If we fail to return to the Lord what already belongs to Him, it will bring a curse on our lives.

If we fail to return to the Lord what already belongs to Him, it will bring a curse on our lives.

Never forget what happened to Cain and Abel, the sons of Adam and Eve. The Bible records, "Now Abel kept flocks, and Cain worked the soil. In the course of time Cain brought some of the fruits of the soil as an offering to the Lord" (Genesis 4:2-3).

Notice the specific wording here. It says "Cain brought *some* of the fruits of the soil..." Contrast this with what we read of his brother's offering: "But Abel brought fat portions from some of the firstborn of his flock. The Lord looked with favor on Abel and his offering, but on Cain and his offering he did not look with favor. So Cain was very angry, and his face was downcast" (verses 4-5).

Cain's "some" is the equivalent of placing a couple of dollars in the offering each Sunday—it has no connection to the level of your blessing the previous week. "First fruits" on the other hand is bringing God the *first* of what crosses your hand.

> ***"First fruits" is bringing God the first of what crosses your hand.***

What was God's reaction to Cain? The Lord asked him, "Why are you angry? Why is your face downcast? If you do what is right, will you not be accepted? But if you do not do what is right, sin is crouching at your door; it desires to have you, but you must master it" (vv.6-7).

Even though Cain gave *something*, God did not consider his offering to be *equal* with what Abel presented. Next, because God accepted Abel's offering, Cain was upset and asked his brother to go out into a field. While they were there, "Cain attacked his brother Abel and killed him" (Genesis 4:8).

Remember, the difference between the offerings of Cain and Abel is that Cain gave "some" while his brother gave from the "first." So tithing is the initial step we must take to have the touch of God upon our lives.

Before I buy a new stereo or make the car payment, I put God first financially. When I pay my bills, the first check I write is that of my tithe. Before anything else, I faithfully take care of my obligation to the Almighty.

With Childlike Faith

A man came to our church who had not had the privilege of being raised in a Christian home. He never attended Sunday school, and knew practically zero about the Bible. He didn't own a Gold American Express card or a huge line of credit. In fact he had sought every solution for his financial problems and still his back was pressed against the wall.

In desperation he came to church and received the message I preached through the anointing of the Holy Spirit. Even more, with childlike faith, he began to tithe and put the principles he heard into practice.

Here's the best part. In five years he grew both spiritually and financially—much more than others who failed to obey God's Word.

The Truth Will Set You Free

In the next chapter, I will share what you can expect when you combine tithing and faith. I believe it will help you reach a new level of understanding.

Jesus said, "You will know the truth, and the truth will set you free." (John 8:32).

God is a loving Father who wants to bless His children. You will discover that the tithe was not instituted to take money *from* you. Just the opposite; it is His way of giving abundance *to* you. God always honors His Word.

FOUR

TITHING IS THE BAR OF FAITH

I absolutely believe in the power of tithing and giving back. My own experience about all the blessings I've had in my life is that the more I give away, the more that comes back. That is the way life works.

– KEN BLANCHARD

High school graduates don't just drive up to the college campus of their choice and announce, "I'm here. I am ready to enroll."

No, there are entry levels to be met and hurdles to cross. It was the same when I was a student at Texas Christian University and also when I received my doctorate. The admission counselors didn't say, "He looks like a good candidate. Let's give him a degree."

Well, God also has high standards to be met before

He places His stamp of approval on your life. One of them is what I call "The bar of faith"—tithing.

Some may argue, "I don't see tithing as one of the Ten Commandments, so it can't be that important."

Not so. God instituted the tithe hundreds of years before Moses came down from Mount Sinai. As we have discussed, it was part of the covenant of Abraham—and is a divine ordinance to this day.

The Marines have a recruiting slogan that includes the words, "If you're good enough to get in."

God has His requirements too—and returning a tenth of all He places in our hand is His bar—His threshold.

SOWING AND REAPING

In today's culture, it's hard to comprehend what it must have been like in Bible times when life revolved around plowing the earth, sowing and reaping, seedtime and harvest. When the crops were gathered it was a time for great rejoicing. And the high point was giving a tithe of those crops to the house of the Lord.

We often lose sight of this because most of us are so removed from the land—driving on concrete roads, living in urban housing, and receiving our paychecks electronically.

In those days, you couldn't tithe until you sold your crops. But when you did, it was a time of celebration. And the bigger the harvest, the more you could give to the Lord. It meant you had a bumper season.

His covenants are still valid and He expects them to be kept.

Everything was visual to the entire community—not like zeros and digits on a computer hard drive.

In the Lord's sight, even though society may have changed, His covenants are still valid and He expects them to be kept.

Faith, Action, and Tithing

Let me share ten principles from God's Word that will help you understand how faith, action, and tithing are linked together in a covenant that brings favor, blessing, and abundance to our lives.

Number 1: Faith by itself, if not accompanied by action, is dead.

The reason far too many Christians have very little materially is because they don't truly believe what the Bible teaches: "Faith by itself, if it is not accompanied by action, is dead" (James 2:17).

You may ask, "Are you trying to tell me that if I live for God and follow His commands there ought to be a material payoff?"

What do you think the covenant of Abraham, Isaac, and Jacob is all about?

You will have great difficulty finding anybody in the Bible who walked with God and was destitute.

From Testing to Trust

The example people often give is Job. Yes, God tested him, and he suffered with boils so painful that while sitting in an ash heap he scraped his skin with broken pottery to ease his agony. But he brought many of his problems on himself because he confessed the very thing that distressed him: "What I feared has come upon me; what I dreaded has happened to me" (Job 3:25).

> ***Job may have plummeted to the depths of despair, but he didn't remain there.***

Job may have plummeted to the depths of despair, but he didn't remain there. He was finally able to truly say, "Though he slay me, yet will I trust in him" (Job 13:15).

If you read the last chapters of the book of Job you'll

find that he ended up with twice as much as he had before his troubles began. And I'm not only referring to his spiritual wealth. "The Lord blessed the latter end of Job more than his beginning: for he had fourteen thousand sheep, and six thousand camels, and a thousand yoke of oxen" (Job 42:12 KJV).

One of the most amazing aspects of this story is that Job persevered even though he wasn't able to tap into the advantages you and I possess today. He had no written Bible to turn to for guidance.

Where is the Fruit?

I've encountered countless men and women who criticize what I believe, but then I stop and think, "What have they produced? Where is the fruit? Where is the evidence in their own life?"

However, if an individual comes along who has generated and demonstrated more spiritual and material success than I have, you can rest assured I am more than interested in hearing what that person has to say.

For example, I hesitate to register for a conference that is led by someone who has no record of achievement. Why should I? What is there to learn? But I am more than willing to listen to a proven leader.

When people add action to their faith, they literally come alive—and others want to be around them.

Number two: We demonstrate our faith by what we do.

When we began our ministry, people literally had to take us at face value that we believed God would bless them if they lived by the Word. But now, it doesn't really require much faith to believe. The evidence is obvious. You can visit our church, look around, and see that faith works.

Those who are watching will know what you believe by your walk, not by your talk.

As I tell people, "Faith shows up!'

Those who are watching will know what you believe by your walk, not by your talk.

James addressed this issue when he wrote, "But someone will say, 'You have faith; I have deeds.' Show me your faith without deeds, and I will show you my faith by what I do" (James 2:18).

THE CAUSE OF DISHARMONY

Over the years, Sue and I have counseled many

married couples. And the number one cause of fights and disharmony in the home is money—or I should say, the lack of it.

Come to think of it, we have never had to counsel a couple because they had so much wealth they didn't know how to spend it!

Why do we allow the devil to talk us into the nonsense that we are not worthy or that we don't deserve abundance? If Satan can destroy our finances, he can wreck our homes.

What Makes the Difference?

When you are born again and join a church where faith is taught, your unbelieving friends hardly know what to think when they start hearing you confessing the Word—"I am the head and not the tail." "I am more than a conqueror."

Behind your back they are snickering.

When you confess healing over your sick child they think you've lost your mind.

But a few years later, when you have moved into a custom brick home, and drive up to the family reunion in your new luxury sedan with a healthy family, they hardly know what to think.

What made the difference? Faith showed up!

MORE THAN LUCK

I've seen it over and over again. Thirty years ago a dear saint of God was making only $10,000 a year, living meagerly, but faithfully tithing on that amount. Their neighbor was making the same money, but instead of tithing, was spending what they couldn't afford on weekend trips and personal pleasures.

Three decades later, the tither had their financial house in order and the spender was still trying to make ends meet.

The average person would look at the tither and say, "Well, he's just lucky." But mere chance had nothing to do with it. God promises to reward those who keep His Word—and He always does.

If faith doesn't show up, there was no faith to begin with.

GIVING GRUDGINGLY

I've met people who brag, "I tithe religiously."

What they mean is, "I really don't like doing this, but since it's in the Bible, I have to." They give grudgingly, as if God is standing over them wielding a big stick, waiting to give them a whack if they fail to obey Him.

It's no wonder such individuals never reap the rewards God promises. There is no faith, no expectation, no joy.

Your tithe is to be given with confession—"Lord I believe and I receive." This is how you will see the thirty, sixty, and one hundred fold blessing Jesus spoke of (Matthew 13:8).

From Duty to Delight

Personally, I love tithing—and the more I can give the happier I am. I really enjoy writing out tithing checks. In fact, the more zeros the better. Why do I say this? Because if I give God $100, it means I have received $1,000. If I write out a $1,000 check, I have taken in $10,000. And one of the most rewarding days of my life is when I wrote out a $10,000 check to the Lord.

> ***The tithe is not a synonym for burden or duty, rather for rejoicing and delight.***

I couldn't wait to present it to Him. After all, it was His, not mine. I was only a steward of the funds for a short period.

The tithe is not a synonym for burden or duty,

rather for rejoicing and delight.

I feel sorry for the man or woman who sits in church thinking, "Let me see how I can avoid doing what the Bible asks." What a disastrous mindset!

What a dynamic difference it makes in the lives of those who eagerly say, "Let me see how I can put God's principles into practice."

There is a supernatural aspect to tithing.

There is a supernatural aspect to tithing. I am convinced that the blessings my wife and I are currently enjoying is not only because of the giving we are doing today, it is the result of the pattern we established years ago.

You see, a giver's life picks up momentum through the years.

BRING IT ON!

God always tries to give as much as He can to His children without spoiling them. And He often offers more than some are willing to receive.

I don't want to be a complainer. In fact, I want God to have the liberty to lay on my life every blessing He desires for me to have. This is not being selfish—it's being smart.

Number 3: Faith without deeds is useless.

If you strip action out of faith, you are left with only belief. You are like the person who states, "I believe if I exercise every day my body would be in better shape." You can believe this for as long as you want, but nothing will change until you exert yourself and step on that treadmill or start lifting weights.

You can desire a happy home, but what are you doing to create one?

Scripture asks, "You foolish man, do you want evidence that faith without deeds is useless? (James 2:20).

Add Faith to Action

I meet couples who continually believe for things that are not possible to receive or achieve in the realm of faith without corresponding action being taken. For example, they want a happy marriage, but do absolutely nothing to keep the spark of romance alive.

Since Sue and I were married, we have done our best to set aside a "date night" once a week. Even when we were young missionaries in Africa and our son Austin was a little boy, we found a babysitter and went out to dinner—even though at times it was quite primitive.

But in the process, our love for each other has flourished and blossomed.

Some may criticize, "That doesn't belong in the realm of faith. It is simply good planning and action."

My response is, "When we are in covenant with God, we don't substitute faith for action, instead we *add* action to our faith."

No More Guilt

One of the biggest payoffs of tithing is that it gets rid of your guilt.

> ***One of the biggest payoffs to tithing is that it gets rid of your guilt.***

When I was growing up in Detroit, my dad always wanted to buy me blue shirts at Sears —because that was what was always on sale. Never any variety. He would bring home the same blue shirt time after time.

During my senior year in high school, I was with my dad at a store and saw a particular shirt I really wanted. I asked him, "What about this one?"

He glanced at the price tag and replied, "No, I'm not buying that."

I looked at him and asked, "What's money for if not to spend?"

Immediately, I could see the anger rise in his face.

Since I had my own job and paid my tithe every week, I pulled out my wallet and bought the shirt myself.

Did that ever feel good!

When you live according to the Word of God, you'll find that the guilt factor is removed from your spending.

Today, the money I have is what's left over after I pay my tithe, my offerings, my taxes, and my investing. I'm free and clear—and there's no problem purchasing what I want to buy.

Number 4: Faith and action work together.

Abraham's faith was made complete by what he did, this means faith without action is incomplete faith. The Bible makes this clear: "Was not our ancestor Abraham considered righteous for what he did when he offered his son Isaac on the altar? You see that his faith and his actions were working together, and his faith was made complete by what he did" (James 2:21-22).

Abraham gave the priest a tenth of his increase. And without this increase there would be no tithe.

If you want to avoid tithing, try living with no income. That doesn't sound too appealing to me.

Since tithing has to do with increase, I believe many are suffering financially because they fail to follow God in this matter. Perhaps it is time for them to revise their budget and make certain it meets the Lord's requirements.

ONE DESSERT AT A TIME

It's surprising what you can do by even making small adjustments in your daily routine. Robert Schuller, pastor of the Crystal Cathedral, decided to spend one year without eating desserts. He lost fifteen pounds!

If you want to know why this worked, try stacking 365 pieces of cake or pie al a mode on a table. You will instantly get the picture.

What we do today determines where we will be next week, next month, and next year. In fact, my financial position is not something that occurred overnight. It is a result of how we decided to order our priorities ten, fifteen, and twenty years ago.

YOU'RE A DEBTOR

One man told me, "The way you talk about tithing

makes me think I'm in debt to God."

"Of course you are," I responded.

I explained to him that if you make money in America you are immediately a debtor because you are required by law to pay taxes. And it is the same in God's Kingdom. The money you make is His—but He offers you a much better arrangement than the government. The state and national taxes will probably cost you about thirty or forty percent, but God only requires ten percent. It's a very good deal!

> ***The earth is the Lord's, and since we reside on His land, we are a debtor to Him.***

If you were to use someone else's property as your own, they would either put you in jail or demand any profits you were making. Remember, the earth is the Lord's, and since we reside on His land, we are a debtor to Him.

YOUR "FREE WILL"

How can it be that for five years in a row a person can have the same prayer request, "Pastor, believe with me that I will get out of debt."

Obviously, they are expecting God to do all the work—while they do nothing.

The Lord will never force you to tithe. From the time

of Adam and Eve in the garden, He gave man what is called "free will"—the ability to make our own decisions.

- You are free to have a happy marriage—or not.
- You are free to succeed in your daily life—or not.
- You are free to honor His Word—or not.

The choice is yours, but there are consequences for making the wrong decision.

5. Faith is made complete by action.

If there were two people who graduated from the same college and worked for the same company for twenty years, how would you determine who had made the most progress? You would look at their title, their salary, their office, and their perks.

The difference is in their performance.

If a farmer sows a 100 acres, he harvests a 100-acre crop. But what if he gets industrious and sows 500 acres? He receives a 500-acre reward. Again, our success is based on our output.

This is scriptural: "You see that his faith and his actions were working together, and his faith was made complete by what he did" (James 2:22).

Many operate at cross purposes, saying one thing and doing the exact opposite. They brag about believing all the promises of the Word, but their behavior tells another story.

THE PERCENTAGE DOESN'T CHANGE

I'm thankful I am a citizen of a country where my tithe can be a legitimate deduction on my income taxes. But even if this were not the case, I would still gladly return God's ten percent to Him.

> ***Many operate at cross purposes, saying one thing and doing the exact opposite.***

The longer I live, the more ten percent is reasonable. Think of it. You can make all you want and the percentage doesn't change. I'm glad the Lord is not a Washington bureaucrat or we would be asked to give on a sliding scale—the more we make the more we pay. But in God's economics, I can make $1 million and still pay only ten percent.

Number six: A person is justified by what he does and not by faith alone.

I know that there are some who will read this

heading and indignantly say, "This is where I close the book. How dare Dr. Lingerfelt suggest that we are not justified by faith alone!"

Well, these are not my words, they are taken directly from the Bible. Here is what James declares: "And the scripture was fulfilled that says, 'Abraham believed God, and it was credited to him as righteousness, and he was called God's friend.' You see that a person is justified by what he does and not by faith alone" (James 2:23-24).

However, if you read those last few words closely you will come to the right conclusion that it is a combination of our faith and our actions—our belief and our behavior—that results in justification.

WHAT'S THE PROBLEM?

There are men and women who firmly believe God will raise their body from the grave, but doubt He can replace ten percent of their income. So tithing isn't the issue—it is symptomatic of a larger root problem.

They profess to believe the Lord, but they spend more on pet food than what they give to missions. They say they believe in heaven, but never lead anyone to a saving knowledge of Christ—or even warn them of an eternal hell.

Once you take a word like "tithe" out of the Bible you feel at liberty to remove anything else you don't like—or add what you think it should include.

You can't do that with your tax returns. There are strict regulations and you had better follow them!

"Prove Me Now"

Be warned. God sets the rules for life, and no one will spend eternity with Him who doesn't abide by His Word.

> ***God sets the rules for life, and no one will spend eternity with Him who doesn't abide by His Word.***

God states, "'Ever since the time of your forefathers you have turned away from my decrees and have not kept them. 'Return to me, and I will return to you,' says the Lord Almighty. 'But you ask, "How are we to return?"' (Malachi 3:7).

Then the Lord explains:

"Will a man rob God? Yet you rob me. But you ask, 'How do we rob you?' In tithes and offerings. You are under a curse—the whole nation of you—because you are robbing me. Bring the whole tithe into the storehouse, that there may be food in my house. Test me in this," says the Lord Almighty, "and see if I will not throw open the floodgates of heaven and pour out so much blessing that you will not have room enough for it. I will prevent pests from devouring your crops, and the vines in your fields will not cast their fruit," says the Lord Almighty. "Then all the nations will call you blessed, for yours will be a delightful land" (verses 8-12).

There can be no doubt. The tithe belongs to God—and if your are withholding it, you are robbing Him.

The tithe belongs to God—and if you are withholding it, you are robbing Him.

Tithing is one of the only aspects of our Christian walk where we are allowed to put God to the test. He says, "Prove me now."

Since He gives you the permission, why not try it?

WHERE SHOULD YOU GIVE?

You have to discipline yourself to plant your finances into good soil. If you give your tithe to your brother-in-law or some other relative, that's not the storehouse God intended. Why? Because it is not where you receive your spiritual food.

And we should never complain when we present our tithe to the Lord because He isn't looking for a fearful or tearful giver—"God loves a cheerful giver" (2 Corinthians 9:7).

God's True Joy

Tithing wasn't instituted because God needed the wealth. All He would have to do is pick up one brick in heaven from a street paved with gold. But He asks us to tithe so we can be blessed for being obedient.

When we neglect giving, we rob God of the joy of granting us His favor.

Even though my wife and I do wonderful things for our children, God does even more.

We have no idea of the power that would be unleashed on earth if every believer would live in lock step with God's Word. The world would take notice and all nations would call us blessed.

Number 7: Tithing is not about money; it is about your heart.

I love these words of Jesus: "But seek first his kingdom and his righteousness, and all these things will be given to you as well" (Matthew 6:33).

The Lord wasn't giving us a choice between "Kingdom" or "things." He is telling us to seek the resources of heaven and the righteousness of God and we won't have to worry about earthly goods. The decision we have to make is, what are we going to put first?

In context, this verse clearly addresses the matter of our daily needs; what we will eat and the clothing we will wear (verses 31-32). But Jesus is telling us there is a better way to satisfy our needs. He is saying, "You can have it all—both the spiritual and the material."

"You can have it all—both the spiritual and the material."

The tither is placing spiritual matters ahead of anything else, but the non-giver lets us know his priorities. He is "things" oriented.

AN "OVERFLOWING" SUPPLY

Scripture explains it this way: "Honor the Lord with your wealth, with the firstfruits of all your crops; then your barns will be filled to overflowing, and your vats will brim over with new wine" (Proverbs 3:9-10).

We may not own barns, but we do have money market accounts and funds in the stock market. If having more than we need is a sin, why would God promise an "overflowing" supply?

Putting God First

Whenever we experience a health or financial hardship, we want God to immediately put us at the head of the line and make us His first priority. But what about us reciprocating, making Him our number one priority by offering Him our "first fruits"?

Please notice they are not called "last fruits."

Tithing is not just about money. It is all about putting God first and seeing the Word work in your life. Tithing is part of the Father's divine plan to bless His people.

The "god" of most Americans is cold hard cash—and it is also true with much of the world. So, when a man or woman sets that first ten percent aside as a tithe, it becomes evident they have embraced the true and living God.

Where is Your Treasure?

Consider what Jesus said in His Sermon on the Mount: "Do not store up for yourselves treasures on earth, where moth and rust destroy, and where thieves break in and steal. But store up for yourselves treasures in heaven, where moth and rust do not destroy, and where thieves do not break in and steal. For where your treasure is, there your heart will be also" (Matthew 6:19-21).

Tithing should be at the very center of your life, because if our treasure is not in the Kingdom, we may be a member of a church, but are a disaster waiting to happen—and anything will distract and veer us off course.

I have never met a man or woman who has made a substantial investment in God's Kingdom and walked away from it. Their "heart" is reflected in their obedience to the Word, and it keeps them connected to heaven.

Number 8: Tithing is not about money; it is about faith.

When I was about five years old, my mother had a medical need. She had two slipped disks in her back.

We had moved from Highland Park to Warren, Michigan, and I remember staying with a neighbor boy while she was in the hospital.

There were to be two operations, but the first one was so painful that she was determined to find a way to avoid going through another surgery. So she began searching for answers. Then one day she turned on the radio and listened to the broadcast of James Beall of Bethesda Missionary Temple in Detroit.

He was teaching on faith and healing, so she decided to start attending that church.

The first thing they taught me in Sunday school was how God loved me so much that He gave His only Son as a sacrifice for my sin. So at the young age of five I gave my life to the Lord.

Next, they taught me the principle of tithing—and that it wasn't a gift to give but a debt to pay. I can still visualize those small Sunday School envelopes we were to use to bring our tithe to the Lord.

> ***I have learned from experience that tithing is not about money, it is about faith.***

My weekly allowance in those days was twenty-five cents. I didn't know how to calculate ten percent of that amount so I always put a nickle in the Sunday School envelope.

I have been a tither since that day forward.

To say I have been blessed is an understatement, and I make no apology for it. I have learned from experience that tithing is not about money, it is about faith. And from the age of five, my faith has continued to multiply and grow.

Seed for the Sower

God helps us by giving us a "starter kit."

"Now he who supplies seed to the sower and bread

for food will also supply and increase your store of seed and will enlarge the harvest of your righteousness" (2 Corinthians 9:10).

For me, my initial test was 25 cents a week—and God wanted to see what I would do with it.

The prophet Isaiah wrote, "As the rain and the snow come down from heaven, and do not return to it without watering the earth and making it bud and flourish, so that it yields seed for the sower and bread for the eater" (Isaiah 55:10).

What is in your hand?

Number 9: Faith demands action.

If you sincerely desire freedom and liberty in your walk with Christ, be a "doer" of the Word. As scripture counsels: "Do not merely listen to the word, and so deceive yourselves. Do what it says" (James 1:22).

When you act upon scripture, the spiritual power in your life will astound your friends and co-workers.

The apostle James gives this analogy: "Anyone who listens to the word but does not do what it says is like a man who looks at his face in a mirror and, after looking at himself, goes away and immediately forgets what he looks like. But the man who looks intently into the perfect law that gives freedom, and continues to do this, not forgetting what he has heard, but doing it—he will be blessed in what he does" (verses 23-24).

Righteous Rahab

James refers to the story of Rahab, the prostitute in the city of Jericho who secretly gave lodging to the spies of Joshua before they overtook the city. She was "considered righteous," for what she did (James 2:25). We also find her listed in the Hall of Faith along with the heroes of the Old Testament (Hebrews 11:31). And she is in the lineage of Jesus (Matthew 1:5).

Her actions inspired James to write: "As the body without the spirit is dead, so faith without deeds is dead" (James 2:26).

God doesn't worry about your background. He can transform your life.

God doesn't worry about your background. He can transform your life. What matters is that your seed is planted with faith in good soil.

Number 10: Tithing is our access to God's covenant blessing.

When the priest Melchizedek blessed Abraham, he

reminded him that he was not being honored because he was a great warrior or had won victories on the battlefield. No, Melchizedek said, "Blessed be God Most High, who delivered your enemies into your hand" (Genesis 14:20).

If any man begins to think he's blessed because he is smart, or a genius, he'd better think again. It is God Almighty who deserves all the praise and glory.

Abraham realized this and immediately gave the Lord his tithe (verse 20). He demonstrated his faith by his actions.

THE BENEFITS ARE REAL

The covenant of tithing connected Abraham to his blessing. This is where faith involved something tangible.

The covenant of tithing connected Abraham to his blessing.

Tithing doesn't bring God into partnership with *us.* Just the opposite. It moves us into an association with *Him.* Afer all, it was the Lord who commanded that His children give a tenth of their income to His work.

The benefits, however, are real. As a result of our giving we have the Father's blessing on our work, on our home, and on our family.

Tithing is fundamental to our faith. But according to a recent Barna Report, only three percent of those who attend church in America tithe; and of evangelical Christians, only eight percent claim to tithe. And these numbers may be high since most people want to make themselves look good to those taking the survey!

Perhaps you have noticed that politicians ingratiate themselves to practically every segment of American society. But they usually steer clear of the Christians. Why? Because they don't have enough money! The above statistics may tell us the reason why.

The Blessings are Yours

When you truly grasp that tithing is a covenant, not a convenience, your entire approach to the matter changes. Remember, "He redeemed us in order that the blessing given to Abraham might come to the Gentiles through Christ Jesus, so that by faith we might receive the promise of the Spirit" (Galatians 3:14). And "If you belong to Christ, then you are Abraham's seed, and heirs according to the promise" (Galatians 3:29).

Tithing is the Bar of Faith

The commandment to tithe is God's way of seeing

who makes the cut. This is where Christianity becomes real.

I believe tithing separates the overcomers from the losers. In the last book of the Bible we find these blunt words, "He who overcomes will inherit all this, and I will be his God and he will be my son. But the cowardly, the unbelieving, the vile, the murderers, the sexually immoral, those who practice magic arts, the idolaters and all liars—their place will be in the fiery lake of burning sulfur. This is the second death" (Revelation 21:7-8).

I believe tithing separates the overcomers from the losers.

John Wayne used to say, "God hates a coward." To put it another way, heaven is not designed for wimps!

A NEVER-ENDING SUPPLY

I love the story of the widow of Zarephath who gave her last morsel of bread to the prophet Elijah. He told her that if she obeyed the Lord, He would give her a never-ending supply of flour and oil.

It took tremendous faith and courage for her to make that decision. But she didn't give just a tenth; she gave all she possessed.

As the result of stepping out in trust and belief, the Bible records, "So there was food every day for Elijah and for the woman and her family. For the jar of flour was not used up and the jug of oil did not run dry, in keeping with the word of the Lord spoken by Elijah" (1 Kings 17:15-16).

What a tremendous payoff for obeying God's prophet!

REMIND HIM OF THE PROMISES

God says, "Put me in remembrance" (Isaiah 43:26 KJV), and this is exactly what I do when I pay my tithe. I remind the Lord of His promises:

- "Give, and it will be given to you. A good measure, pressed down, shaken together and running over, will be poured into your lap. For with the measure you use, it will be measured to you" (Luke 6:38).

- "And my God will meet all your needs according to his glorious riches in Christ Jesus (Philippians 4:19).

- "You will be made rich in every way so that you can be generous on every occasion, and through us your generosity will result in thanksgiving to God" (2 Corinthians 9:11).

- "With man this is impossible, but not with God; all things are possible with God" (Mark 10:27).

Tithing and giving God what belongs to Him is where faith is proven.

What are you doing about what you say you believe? Have you passed the bar of faith?

FIVE

THE POWER OF THE SECOND "TENTH"

A penny saved is a dollar earned.

– BENJAMIN FRANKLIN

When Sue and I returned to the United States in 1983 from serving as missionaries in Africa, we had very little financially—about $20,000 in equity from the sale of our first home. We plowed that money into starting the church we now pastor.

Yes, we preached faith and I confessed the promises of God's Word that He wanted me to be the head not the tail, and to prosper in all things. But I have to admit that I was complaining to Him regarding our lack of financial resources.

Then one day in prayer the Lord clearly spoke to me: "You don't have any money because you never *save* any money."

God gave me this word of instruction: "Save

something every seven days, even if it is only five dollars."

The Lord was telling me, "How can I bless you if you spend more than you make?"

So, starting in 1989, I began saving at least *something* every week. Within two years I had reworked my budget so that I was able to save or invest at least 10 percent of my income—and I have never fallen below that level.

During one of those years, I received a raise. But I told my wife, "We're not going spend any of this increase. It is all going into savings."

FINANCIAL MIRACLES

I finally reached the 80-10-10 benchmark. The 80 percent was mine to spend, 10 percent belonged to God, and I either saved or invested the last 10 percent.

I firmly believe that because I was faithful, both spiritually and materially, God allowed financial miracles to come my way. For example, in 1991, just two years after making my life-changing commitment, I became involved in a home transaction where the buying price was so drastically reduced that it resulted in a $150,000 equity windfall. And not long after this, another opportunity presented itself with an even larger reward.

I am not revealing this information to brag, but within four years after God gave me His instruction, I was a millionaire. This is why I can personally tell you the 80-10-10 plan really works.

It's not just because you are saving and investing money. There is a greater factor at work. When you are being totally obedient to God's work regarding both tithing and investing, you are giving the Lord something to bless, and He places His favor on whatever you put your hand to.

A Lack of Knowledge

The earlier in life you adopt this pattern, the more time you have for saving and investing. Personally, Sue and I got off to a slow start because nobody ever told us the things I am sharing with you now.

Sue and I got off to a slow start because nobody ever told us the things I am sharing with you now.

I received straight A's in algebra but my teachers never taught me about compound interest.

They might give you a math problem such as: "If you are driving fifty miles an hour and your destination is forty miles ahead, how long will it take you to get there?"

Never once did a teacher ask, "If you save $100 a month and it grows at 10% interest, how long will it take for you to be a millionaire?"

Those kinds of problems were not presented.

In addition, my father never had a talk with me about investing or encouraged me to start a savings plan. For whatever reason, it was a subject that was never broached.

My wife's dad was the same. Even though he was an investor, he never told her why she should follow in his footsteps.

The reason so many reach their twilight years without adequate resources is because (1) no one ever explained the power of saving or investing or (2) they lack will power.

THE FIVE DOLLAR MILLIONAIRE

Saving and investing is far easier than most people realize.

If you drive to your neighborhood Starbucks, order a cappuccino and a muffin, you'll probably spend five bucks. And some individuals do this every day!

Well, what would happen if, at the age of 20, you

gave up that five dollars (about $150 a month) and invested it—and continued doing this every day until you were 65?

Even if you didn't do any research and invested that amount in the Standard & Poor's 500, at age 65 you would have accumulated over $1.5 million.

The decision to save money is yours alone.

What about $10 a day? You'd have about $3.1 million. And $15 per day would produce $4.7 million by the time you retire. That's a boatload of money!

Even factoring in the recessions and market downturns, the stock market (with dividends included) over time averages a 10% annual increase.

The decision to save money is yours alone. Nobody is going to force you.

A Biblical Teaching

Years ago I came to the realization that people needed teaching in this area. Since Jesus spent much of His time speaking on the subject of money, I came to the conclusion that the biblical principles of finances should be taught in the church—right along with faith, salvation, baptism, evangelism, forgiveness, grace,

God's will, and eternity.

> ***In our generation, preaching the "good news to the poor" has come to mean socialism and the redistribution of wealth.***

In the Jewish synagogue at Nazareth, Jesus stood and declared what Isaiah had written centuries earlier: "The Spirit of the Lord is on me, because he has anointed me to preach good news to the poor. He has sent me to proclaim freedom for the prisoners and recovery of sight for the blind, to release the oppressed, to proclaim the year of the Lord's favor" (Luke 4:18-19).

In our generation, preaching the "good news to the poor" has come to mean socialism and the redistribution of wealth.

THE "SOCIAL GOSPEL"

When I attended seminary, there were many who believed in the "social gospel." Their goal was not to bring people to a saving knowledge of Christ, but to find a way to take from those who have more and give to those who have less.

Instead of instructing men and women how to be

self-sufficient and build assets, the emphasis was on taking money from the producers and giving it to those who didn't produce.

This becomes a disincentive for the entrepreneur, who soon comes to the conclusion, "Why should I make any more money if the government is going to take it away from me?"

This also results in the delinquency of those who fail to be productive. They develop a welfare philosophy of life that is handed down from generation to generation.

What a novel idea—training young people how to make money!

LIFTING THE POOR OUT OF POVERTY

What would be "good news" to the less fortunate? Should we say "God wants you to be poor"?

No. The message of Jesus in Luke 4 was that man didn't have to stay in his poverty. He didn't tell the prisoner "I love you, but you will have to remain in prison." No, He brought freedom.

The Lord didn't say to the blind, "I love you, even with your blindness." Instead, He brought recovery and sight.

Why do we think that the "good news" Jesus brought to the poor was only spiritual? If we put it into the proper context, He came to lift the poor out of their poverty so they could prosper materially.

A DREAM REWARDED

When we look at the life of Joseph, "the dreamer," we find that abundance is the will of God for His children:

- Joseph was thrown into a pit by his jealous brothers—but he didn't stay there.
- He was sold into slavery in Egypt—but soon became master of the house where he served.
- He was sentenced to prison on false allegations—yet was soon placed in charge of the prisoners.
- He was freed—by interpreting Pharaoh's dream.
- He was rewarded—and appointed the governor of Egypt.

In the end, God used Joseph to control the resources of Egypt, the greatest empire of the day—and to save Israel from starvation. The time finally came when Joseph was able to tell his brothers, "You intended to harm me, but God intended it for good to accomplish what is now being done, the saving of many lives" (Genesis 50:20).

Will Your Ship Come In?

Some people dream for years about landing on Easy Street—but they never do anything about it.

One man told me, "I'm still waiting for my ship to come in."

How could that ever happen when he never sent a ship out to sea! If you don't have a vessel called "investment," it will never return full.

> ***People who are the biggest critics are usually the smallest givers.***

I observed long ago that people who are the biggest critics are usually the smallest givers. But those who are investors—whether it be in a business or a church—long to see the project succeed. So instead of finding fault, they want to encourage, build, and see things prosper.

Stick With the Plan

The practice of investing is much like losing weight. It's not very exciting at the beginning. The person who has eighty pounds to shed may step on the scales after a few days and find he has only lost one pound. This is one-eightieth of his goal and can be discouraging. But look what happens if you consistently stick with the game plan. The weight starts falling off, your confidence and motivation builds, and you finally see dramatic results.

In our fast-food, quick-delivery society, when it finally dawns on people that they'd better start investing, they want immediate returns. These individuals would rather skip the verse that reads, "He who gathers money little by little makes it grow" (Proverbs 13:11).

I know men and women who make a half-million dollars a year, yet never save one penny. They think their income will keep pouring in for the rest of their life, so they spend it all.

One day they may have a rude awakening!

NEVER TOUCH YOUR SAVINGS

When you become serious and decide on a savings plan, stick to it no matter what.

You may ask, "But what about emergencies?"

To me, this is what credit is for. Let's say your car won't pass inspection unless you immediately purchase a new set of tires. My advice is not to touch your savings. Instead, use a credit card and pay the debt off as fast as humanly possible.

Imagine there is a huge wall or barrier built between your savings and money available on credit. Don't mix the two. If you were to use your savings to pay off debt, you would have a setback in the compound interest of your savings and ten years down the road it would make a noticeable difference in what you accumulate.

> ***Imagine there is a huge wall or barrier built between your savings and money available on credit.***

Your goal is to see your savings grow and your debt decrease. Work on them separately.

Great Decisions Will Cover Poor Mistakes

Regarding investing, I do three things. (1) I plan, (2), I take action, and (3) I speak the scriptures where God has promised to bless the work of my hands.

I'll readily admit I have made some lousy decisions along the way, but I have learned that one great investment decision will cover four or five mistakes. Yet in the process I continually tell the Lord I have His wisdom in me and He is performing His work and His Word in my life.

DON'T SELF-SABOTAGE YOUR OBJECTIVE

If you practice investing for the long haul, you will never have to worry about recession. In fact, you will learn to love it when the market goes down. During this time you are buying more shares for the same amount of money. Then when the economy rebounds—which it always does—you'll own more shares at a much higher value.

After years of investing I have discovered that the more trades I make in a year, the worse I do. The charges and fees for transactions add up and I end up self-sabotaging my objectives.

The phrase "Cash is king" should not be ignored.

There are certain situations, however, when you will need to make decisions regarding how your investments are allocated. In times of recession, as we had in the early eighties and in 2008/2009, your net worth may not be able to keep you above water because your assets decrease in value. The only thing that will pull you through is cash. This is why you should always have money market accounts available—or be alert enough to convert other investments to cash at the start of a downfall. The phrase "Cash is king," should not be ignored.

After studying the market for fifteen years, the best advice I know of is this: When the 50-day moving average on the *Standard & Poor 500* crosses below the 200-day moving average, it is best to get out for safety's sake.

The reverse is also true. In a downturn, the market may go through many ups and downs, but when the 50-day moving average crosses above the 200-day moving average on the *Standard & Poor 500*, the long term trend is back up. To reach your long term goals you will need to get back in the market.

Life does not consist of just spring and summer. As we recently experienced, the world's economic climate can drastically change. There will be fall and winter, and it is our cash that will tide us over.

Use Withholding to Your Advantage

Until the Civil War there was no income tax in the United States. They used tariffs on imports to pay the cost of government. But to finance the war, they passed the Revenue Act of 1861 that called for a 3 percent tax on all annual earnings over $800.

The problem was that no one wanted to pay their taxes and collections were a huge problem. Eventually some bureaucrat came up with a very clever solution. It was called "withholding"—enacted during World War II.

The idea was that if taxes were taken from weekly or monthly paychecks, people wouldn't feel the pain so much. It worked!

Today, if the system didn't exist and every American were asked to write out a check on April 15 for the total amount of the previous year's taxes, there would be rebellion in the streets! The government wouldn't be fearing Al Qaeda—they would be afraid of angry citizens at home.

The same principle of withholding, however, can be used to your advantage in this positive area of savings. You can have a set amount automatically transferred to a money market account or a mutual fund and you'll forget it is even happening. Meanwhile that money is working on your behalf.

FREE MONEY!

Never ever turn "free money" away.

> ***Never ever turn "free money" away.***

A man in my church told me, "For every dollar I put into a savings plan, my company will add fifty cents. Should I do it?"

I wanted to slap him on the head! "Of course you should do it. That is free money!"

The answer is the same when your firm offers to pay for college courses. Take them up on it immediately. Not only will they see you as a long term employee, but you will likely receive a promotion when you get your degree.

What About Your Children?

Whatever goal you set for yourself, you can reach it as long as your don't run out of time.

This is why you need to take care of your body—so it remains healthy and lasts longer; it is the house you live in. If your years are shortened, you won't be able to give your children what you desire for them to have financially.

Remember, investing is not all about you, it concerns your sons, your daughters, and your grandchildren. The Bible tells us, "A good man leaves an inheritance for his children's children" (Proverbs 13:22).

It's a shame that every Christian generation seems to start over from scratch because so few have ever been taught to save anything financially. Sadly, many parents can't even help their children receive a college education because they lack financial discipline.

Make Your Commitment Now

You have no idea how dramatically your life will

change for the better when you commit yourself to tithing, plus saving an additional ten percent. Because of your obedience, God will open the windows of heaven and pour out unexpected blessings.

Promise the Lord and yourself that you will start setting aside that "tenth" today.

SIX

THE MULTIPLICATION FACTOR

Put not your trust in money, but put your money in trust.

– OLIVER WENDELL HOLMES

A century ago a sharecropper would go to the store to buy his seed—usually on credit to be paid for when the crops came in. Then he would have to give a portion of what he harvested to the land owner. In many cases, the same man owned both the farm and the store—so he received a cut of everything!

We like to think that things have progressed and changed, but have they really?

The objective of both government and commerce is to keep you in debt, because this is what causes you to get up and go to work in the morning.

In fact, many politicians love the fact that family income has been squeezed to the point that women have been forced to enter the workplace. More taxes for Washington!

THE BONDAGE OF INTEREST

Don't forget credit card companies. They do everything in their power to rope you into bondage early. The reason they only want you to pay the minimum monthly payment is because the interest rates are so exorbitant you'll be paying on the card for the rest of your life!

I recently purchased a car and set up a monthly payment schedule because I don't like touching the money that is in savings. About a month and a half later I wrote out a check and paid off the vehicle in full.

Within a few days the bank called me—and I can tell you they weren't happy. You see, the profit from interest is the only reason they are financing cars. I told the loan officer, "Did I miss something? Was there a prepayment penalty?"

He hesitated, and replied, "Well, no."

"Then what's the problem?" I wanted to know.

He had no answer.

I didn't want to tell him, but I had that "prepayment anointing" on me!

Cash to Spend

There is something inherently wrong going on in America. Compared to most other nations our household savings rate is anemic.

If you travel to Paris and walk into a high end store, you will find plenty of Chinese and Japanese tourists buying practically everything in sight. Why? Because the savings rates of their countries are among the highest on the planet. They have cash to spend.

Those who consume everything and have no savings plan are not being fair—either to themselves or to their family.

> ***Continuing to budget so there is "just enough" is a high-risk strategy.***

Continuing to budget so there is "just enough" is a high-risk strategy. How will you handle the unexpected—such as when your air conditioner compressor breaks down, or your refrigerator goes on the blink? If you don't have a nest egg set aside, how will you replace them?

Since you regularly pay the electric company, the car note, and the mortgage payment, doesn't it make sense to pay yourself?

Do not be unwise and copy the locust and consume all you have.

Saving money is a biblical principle: "In the house of

the wise are stores of choice food and oil, but a foolish man devours all he has" (Proverbs 21:20).

IS BORROWING SCRIPTURAL?

Since I believe so strongly in saving and investing, you may wonder, "What about borrowing?"

When we built our first church building, it was necessary to borrow funds for its completion and one member became upset and left the church.

On the way out the door he said, "I don't believe it's biblical to borrow. We are not to owe any man—and that includes churches borrowing from banks."

It is true that scripture tells us, "You will lend to many nations but will borrow from none" (Deuteronomy 28:12). But if borrowing is wrong, why would God tell us it is permissible to lend? Would He deliberately cause someone to sin?

The apostle Paul counseled, "Let no debt remain outstanding, except the continuing debt to love one another" (Romans 13:8). Instead of a prohibition against borrowing, it is an admonition to pay our obligations.

The gentleman who didn't think it was proper to borrow money also did not believe it was God's will to *save* money. He thought Philippians 4:19 meant God would always supply every need he had. Even more outlandish, the man didn't believe it was right to own life insurance.

In my opinion, he was not only hindering the work of God, but jeopardizing his own family.

By the way, we paid off that fifteen year note on our first church building in seven years. So, yes, we borrowed, but then we accelerated the payoff schedule and thus increased the net worth of the church. How did we accomplish such a goal? By not spending every nickel we took in!

A Barrier to Growth

There are times when obtaining a loan is absolutely necessary, even though we would be better off without the debt.

I know a pastor who is totally committed to not borrowing money. His congregation outgrew their present facility ten years ago and their growth is stymied because of his position on the matter. In my opinion, the pastor is a barrier to the growth of God's work.

What if you never purchased a home until you could pay cash? What neighborhood would you be living in?

Debt is not sinful, but it certainly must be utilized intelligently.

Debt is not sinful, but it certainly must be utilized intelligently.

WILLING AND OBEDIENT

To me, saving and investing is not a problem of "can't"—it's a problem of "won't."

It is sad but true that many Christians have been taught how to both think and talk "poor," but it is the will of God for you to prosper—and He has a plan to make this happen.

> ***To me, saving and investing is not a problem of "can't"—it is a problem of "won't."***

The Lord promises, "If you are willing and obedient, you will eat the best from the land" (Isaiah 1:19). So obviously God approves of you driving the best car, living in the best house, and wearing the best clothes.

Some are obedient, but not willing. Others are willing, but not obedient. Both virtues are required.

"BUY LAND"

There are dozens of investment strategies and I recommend many of them, but recently a young couple asked me, "We have accumulated a few thousand dollars. What do you think we should do with it?"

Without hesitation, I told them, "Buy land."

"What land?" they wanted to know.

"Any land," I responded. "The reason it almost always goes up in value is because God isn't creating any more of it."

There is a reason that real estate is called "real." It involves something tangible—something concrete.

The rule of investing is "Buy low and sell high." This is why buying is more important than selling. If what you purchase is a true bargain, you will not get hit too hard when it comes time to sell—whether it be cars, coins, collectibles, common stock, or a condo.

THE $18 MILLION CHECK

You will never reach your financial objective on a hope, a promise, a prayer, and a confession. While all these certainly help, you need a specific blueprint—and the fortitude to stay with the plan. As Solomon stated, "He who works his land will have abundant food, but the one who chases fantasies will have his fill of poverty" (Proverbs 28:19).

Several years ago a man gave our church a "faith" check for $18 million. I still have it. Of course it was no good, just somebody's pipe dream—or maybe he ate too much pizza!

GET RICH QUICK?

There is a huge difference between being a wealth builder and simply seeking instant riches.

In my observation, Christians are far too susceptible to get-rich-quick schemes. Those who have a mindset that their coffers are going to be full overnight open themselves up to unscrupulous, crafty people. But remember, "A stingy man is eager to get rich and is unaware that poverty awaits him" (Proverbs 28:22).

It is both foolish and not Christlike to be naive and fall for gimmicks.

Those who seek money for its own sake are walking on shaky ground.

Making a profit and acquiring wealth legitimately is one thing, but seeking to get rich by clever tactics is quite another. There is a different attitude, a different spirit involved. As the Bible says, "Cast but a glance at riches, and they are gone, for they will surely sprout wings and fly off to the sky like an eagle" (Proverbs 23:5).

Those who seek money for its own sake are walking on shaky ground. The apostle Paul addressed this issue when he wrote to young Timothy: "People who want to get rich fall into temptation and a trap and into many foolish and harmful desires that plunge men into ruin and destruction. For the love of money is a root of all kinds of evil" (1 Timothy 6:9-10).

WHAT IS YOUR SOURCE?

Make certain your priorities are in order. Your love for the Lord comes first—far ahead of seeking material blessings.

Jesus warned, "No one can serve two masters. Either he will hate the one and love the other, or he will be devoted to the one and despise the other. You cannot serve both God and money" (Matthew 6:24).

You are serving the Lord—and obeying Him—when it comes to increasing your finances so you can support both your family and God's work.

Wall Street is not my source, because what Wall Street giveth it can also take away. The Internet is not my source, because it takes more than knowledge to make wise decisions.

When all is said and done, I have to acknowledge that God alone is my source.

THREE BARRIERS

I firmly believe that becoming a millionaire in America should be the norm. But there are three reasons most people never reach this level: (1) they don't allow time to work for them, (2) they accumulate too much debt, and (3) they neglect their marriage.

> ***The average millionaire in the United States has been married for 38 years.***

The average millionaire in the United States has been married for 38 years. This is a lengthy time. But it also reflects the fact that there is stability in the home.

You can't just periodically give up half your assets in a divorce proceeding and expect to keep your financial plan on course. This is one more reason you need to protect and guard your covenant of marriage.

THE POWER OF CONSISTENCY

I would be lying if I told you that it only takes faith for your dreams to come true. No, it also requires knowledge, wisdom, planning, action, and consistency.

You have to be patient and watch your investments grow stronger over time.

It's the same with marriage. You and your spouse may have an occasional argument, but it is the power of love nurtured through the years that cements and builds an unbreakable bond.

If you are consistently doing the right thing, a minor mistake or detour will not be disastrous.

The person who works 50 hours a week, 50 weeks a

year is entitled to a two week vacation. But if you work two weeks and take 50 off, you will quickly find yourself in deep trouble.

It's the same with investing. What are you doing *most* of the time? Let me repeat; making money is doing the right thing consistently over time.

Look at the Numbers

I keep urging people to make an early start. When they do, the numbers are in their favor.

Let's say a young man finds a job at the age of eighteen that pays only $20,000 a year. Even though he has no college education and starts at this low wage, he sets aside 10 percent of what he makes each year and averages a 5 percent raise annually. With the normal 10 percent historic stock market average increase, by the time he is 65 years old he will be worth $3.7 million.

This is why I say that every American should retire a millionaire.

"The Eighth Wonder"

The secret of wealth accumulation is the factor called "compound interest." When the interest you earn on an investment is added to the principle, you now have a larger dollar amount.

British banking magnate Barron Rothschild once observed, "Compound interest is the eighth wonder of the world." And Albert Einstein called it "The most powerful force in the universe."

Just like throwing a stone in the pond, it ripples outward and becomes larger.

If you want to know how good an investment might be, try using what is called "The Rule of 72." To find the number of years it takes to double your money, simply divide the interest rate into 72. For example, if the interest rate is 8 percent it would take 9 years. If your return is 12 percent it will take 6 years.

TAKE OUT YOUR CALCULATOR

Just as interest applies to the money you invest, it also affects the money you spend.

Take out your calculator before making any major financial decisions.

When I was a boy, home mortgages were generally about 10 years in length, They went to 20 and 30 year mortgages. And right before the 2007 housing market peak you could find 40 year plans.

Let's look at the difference. If you purchased a $300,000 home at 6 percent interest for ten years, your total interest would be $99,674. On a 20 year mortgage, you would pay $215,830. For 30 years, the interest would amount to $347,515. But if you took out one of those 40 year mortgages, you would be paying a whopping $492,308 in interest.

Let me ask: are you willing to shell out an extra $392,634 for the same home (the difference between a 10 year and a 40 year plan)? Even with a 30 year mortgage, you will have paid more than *double* for your house!

Take out your calculator before making any major financial decisions.

A Workable Plan

This is how one family invests in their offspring.

When each child or grandchild is born they file for a Social Security number and open up a brokerage account for that infant. At every birthday from age one through 18 they invest $2,000 a year. Even though they invest $36,000, with compound interest it amounts to a hefty sum. This is truly a case where wealth is inherited from parents (Proverbs 19:14).

If each child keeps adding the same amount after 18 until they are 65, at average interest rates they will have $8.8 million for retirement.

Those who follow this plan could be bluebloods. But very few do, because they would rather spend every penny on themselves now.

DIVINE INSTRUCTION

Yes, I practice the power of faith. I believe that next year will be greater than last year and that "a sinner's wealth is stored up for the righteous" (Proverbs 13:22).

In His Word, God tells me to work, and I do. He tells me to save, and I save. The Lord tells me to invest, and I comply with His instruction. This is how I have been mightily blessed.

By following God's divine plan, I can guarantee that your future will be gloriously transformed.

SEVEN

YOUR OFFERING IS A SEED

We make a living by what we get, but we make a life by what we give.

– WINSTON CHURCHILL

What I am about to share launches the 80-10-10 plan into orbit.

We know that God requires His tithe be returned to Him—10 percent of everything we earn. And we also have learned the dynamic principle of saving or investing the next 10 percent so that our personal wealth will grow.

We are left with 80 percent—ours to spend as we please. However, scripture gives us clear direction as to how at least some of our money is to be used.

When Jesus was speaking to the Pharisees and they

tried to trick Him by asking whether He should pay taxes to the Roman government, Jesus replied, "Give to Caesar what is Caesar's, and to God what is God's" (Matthew 22:21).

This raises the question, "What belongs to God?"

Look closely at what the Almighty said through the prophet Malachi. When asked, "How do we rob You?" the Lord answered, "In tithes and offerings" (Malachi 3:8).

The tithe is what turns the engine on; offerings are what pushes the accelerator to the floor!

These are two distinct forms of giving. The tithe is God's requirement, while offerings—over and above the tithe—are an amount of our choosing, but still expected by our heavenly Father.

It is this second form of giving that transforms abundance into *super*-abundance.

Here's how I explain the difference. The tithe is what turns the engine on; offerings are what pushes the accelerator to the floor!

A Collection in Advance

Throughout the Bible we see offerings being used as part of God's plan. In the Old Testament it was often in the form of placing a sacrifice on the altar. In the New Testament, offerings were received to further the message of Christ and His Kingdom.

For example, Paul, writing to the believers at Corinth, urged them to collect an offering in advance, so the work of the Lord could expand.

Paul wrote, "Each man should give what he has decided in his heart to give, not reluctantly or under compulsion" (2 Corinthians 9:7). And he further told them, "You will be made rich in every way so that you can be generous on every occasion, and through us your generosity will result in thanksgiving to God" (verse 11).

ENLARGING THE HARVEST

The giving of offerings into the Gospel is based on the principle of sowing and reaping.

Look again at what scripture has to say concerning increasing our store of seed: "Now he who supplies seed to the sower and bread for food will also supply and increase your store of seed and will enlarge the harvest of your righteousness" (2 Corinthians 9:10).

I have never seen this be successful for someone who was not first a tither. Once a believer knows this truth, they will not only tithe, but begin sowing offerings into God's Kingdom through seed faith.

"ABOVE AND BEYOND"

By following the 80-10-10 principle, what I earn from investments is enough to create a positive cash flow. Then, because my *store* of seed has increased, I am able to give offerings to the Lord's work—and they become larger and larger gifts over time.

Those who don't give are always praying for an unexpected windfall, but if you make a commitment to practice what you have learned in this book, you will enjoy the abundance God talks about. Then, when a financial miracle comes your way—and it will if you are sowing offerings into the Gospel—what you receive is pure, unadulterated gravy! It won't have to be used to pay past debt or get you out of a financial jam. It's "above and beyond" what you need or expect.

Offerings are how we sow the seeds now to live in overflow later.

MAKE YOUR COMMITMENT

Just because someone, somewhere has a covenant of increase with God doesn't mean you automatically fall under the same umbrella. You must establish and enter into an accord for yourself.

Covenants are not "general" understandings that are all-encompassing. Rather, they are individual—between the two parties who enter into the agreement.

I am convinced that because believers fail to enter into a covenant of seed faith with God, they flounder financially, borrow too much money, and are reduced to seeking financial miracles.

> ***Get alone with God and enter into a divine seed faith agreement with Him.***

Right now, even before you finish reading this book, get alone with God and enter into a divine seed faith agreement with Him. Tell your heavenly Father the commitment you are making regarding both your tithe and your offerings. Only then can you claim the promises of His rewards for your obedience.

"Increase Our Faith"

Jesus continually likened faith to a seed planted which produces desirable and predictable results. He taught, "I tell you the truth, if you have faith as small as a mustard seed, you can say to this mountain, 'Move from here to there' and it will move. Nothing will be impossible for you" (Matthew 17:20).

The point is not the seed, it is the faith. In fact it makes no difference what kind of seed you are talking about, the same principle applies. The Lord could have mentioned any example—from mustard to a watermelon.

The lesson is: it takes faith to move mountains.

On another occasion, Jesus used a similar illustration, but the object wasn't a mountain; it was a mulberry tree.

The disciples were asking the Lord: "Increase our faith!"

He replied, "If you have faith as small as a mustard seed, you can say to this mulberry tree, 'Be uprooted and planted in the sea,' and it will obey you" (Luke 17:6).

Faith is not released until you plant a seed.

Jesus taught this principle wherever He went. Faith is a seed sown and an action taken—and faith is not released until you plant a seed.

To many people, faith and the Word are hit and miss propositions. But there's no chance to it. Jesus was trying to show us how to control and direct our faith at all times.

If we truly believe in either mountain or mulberry-tree-moving faith, we would all rush to be givers.

"According to their Kinds"

Visit any garden store and you will see a selection of seed packets. Even though they are dormant, each has power, but the power is in their potential.

Only when the seed is introduced to the soil and watered will it spring to life. It will sprout and germinate just like the picture on the packet.

This basic law of God was established from the very beginning. The Creator spoke, and: "The land produced vegetation: plants bearing seed according to their kinds and trees bearing fruit with seed in it according to their kinds" (Genesis 1:12).

To this day, tomato seeds produce tomatoes and apple seeds produce apple trees.

This is what makes life predictable.

A Certain Outcome

The law of the harvest is not a mystery. The farmer knows exactly what he plants and reaps accordingly. And if you look around the earth at any given time it is always in production. What is planted in the spring will come up in the fall.

But remember, a man reaps what he sows—and so

we are in charge of our harvest.

If farmers sow certain seed to produce a certain result, why can't we use our faith to have a predictable outcome every time?

We can since the Word never lies!

GIVING IS NOT A ONE-TIME EVENT

You cannot expect a harvest if you never plant a seed.

Faith resembles an explosive device. It has powerful potential, but must be detonated. It is also like a muscle; the more you use it the stronger it becomes. In fact, I would rather have a little faith and release it than have great faith and hold it back.

When I give an offering, I am letting go of my faith and believe that what I expectantly ask of God I will receive.

Today, I am reaping a harvest I can hardly keep up with because giving has become a lifestyle. It flows from my heart and is part of who I am.

BREAK OUT OF THE BOX

I smiled when I heard Oral Roberts say, "The number

one key to success is choosing your parents wisely!"

But what if you have overly-frugal parents? You have to break out of that uncomfortable box.

> ***"The number one key to success is choosing your parents wisely!"***

Once I was in a restaurant and saw a man leave a tip. As he and his wife were about to walk out of the door, she returned to the table and put the money in her purse. I could hardly believe my eyes!

People need to rise above such a penny-pinching level. Yes, life may be challenging financially, but I feel sorry for those who constantly whine and complain about the price of gas, the cost of utilities, and tax increases. It costs what it costs, so instead of griping, get motivated to make more.

FORGIVE THE PAST

Perhaps you grew up in a home where your parents were not generous by nature. They may have even put a guilt trip on you, constantly complaining about what it cost to clothe and feed you.

You must throw those memories overboard. By all means, love your earthly parents for who they are, but you have a heavenly Father who desires to bless you with abundance.

I tell people to stop feeling guilty for living at a higher lifestyle than their parents. If you have been taught that poverty was a sign of godliness, either by your mom, dad, or a pastor, forgive them. That's all they knew.

> ***Because you understand God's plan for giving and receiving, you have changed your outlook.***

But because you understand God's plan for giving and receiving, you have changed your outlook. You now embrace a lifestyle of generosity.

LET GO!

You need to let go before you can move on. If you are always dredging up the past, you will be trapped in a spirit that is contrary to what God intends. He wants you to have an attitude of generosity.

Allow me to speak directly to parents. You may disagree with me, but I am firmly against parents asking their children to pay rent. They didn't ask to be born and grow up in your home. If they volunteer to help you in any way, this is their decision and an added blessing, but it shouldn't be forced on them.

Both my wife and I are generous with our children

because we want the Lord to be generous with us.

At the end of the day, how do you wish to be remembered?

Release It!

Our actions and words are both seed—and they are going to produce a harvest, whether good or bad.

So we need to make an evaluation. Do I want a harvest based on my present behavior or the words I say? If the answer is "no," you had better make a change.

I pray it will penetrate your spirit that it is not how much faith you possess, it is a matter of releasing the faith you have. And there are many ways this is accomplished.

One of the best avenues is through confession—by saying out loud what you believe. In the process, your words become seed.

You can also plant seed faith through an act of mercy or kindness. This will produce results in your marriage, in raising children, and in your business.

Keep All the Channels Open

Today, I am always looking for opportunities to sow

seed on *top* of my seed. So when I present an offering to the Lord, I give it in faith that every aspect of my life will be impacted. I never know exactly how the Lord will bless me, so I keep all the channels open.

This is why I keep sowing and sowing.

What future does a farmer have if he stops planting altogether? Just because he has one bad year is no reason to give up. He knows that if he quits sowing he will have no future at all.

As a church, we give generously to missions and ministry outreach because we are like the farmer. If we don't sow, we're sunk!

There are those who say. "I'll give when the Holy Spirit speaks to me."

Well, some people are so thick-headed and spiritually deaf, I wonder how they ever hear Him!

KEEP IT FLOWING

Regarding giving offerings to the Lord, I don't want to be a reservoir, I want to be a mighty, rushing river.

In your home, if there is a blockage in your kitchen sink do you stop using water? Of course, not. You call a plumber and have the pipe cleaned out so the water can keep flowing.

I am convinced that by continually giving to the

Lord, it increases supply and creates a larger cash flow. And the more I give, the more He expands my "store" of seed.

To me, there would be nothing worse than seeing a wonderful opportunity to give and not have the ability to do so. I'm glad I followed the Lord's command in both tithes and offerings. As a result I have been "made rich in every way" (2 Corinthians 9:11).

I pray you will begin sowing into God's Kingdom through offerings that are not miserly, but generous.

It requires releasing your faith in seed form into His anointed work.

EIGHT

GET READY FOR THE HARVEST

If a person gets his attitude toward money straight, it will help straighten out almost every other area in his life.

– BILLY GRAHAM

When I was a boy, we would often drive to visit my grandparents on their 180-acre farm in Tennessee.

Grandpa grew corn, but his acreage wasn't large enough to compete with the huge agri-business operations. So he switched to specialty corn—a variety that was especially good for the making of popcorn.

Some seasons he had a bumper crop, while in other years it was lean. But every fall he would put the best of his crop in a corn crib. Actually, it was a small barn that was used to store the seed for next year's planting.

It didn't matter how big or small the harvest was, he would not eat or sell the corn he was saving. Why? Because that seed was their future!

Some years he would have to take a job in a nearby town to earn enough money to make it through.

I have very fond childhood memories of when my grandparents would let me use a .22 rifle to hit cans off fence posts. Actually, I was a rather good shot.

Then one day my grandma suggested, "Why don't you take the rifle down to the corn crib. I'll give you a dime for every rat's tail you come back with."

What fun! And I made a few dollars in the process.

In reality, grandma was not only keeping me busy, she was protecting her future. She didn't want those pesky rats eating up next year's profits!

NO FAVORITISM

The farmer is in control of both the quality and the quantity of the crops he plants. My grandpa may have owned 180 acres, but it was his decision whether to plant 10 acres—or all 180.

One thing is sure. The soil doesn't care if the farmer is black or white, tall or short, fat or thin, Presbyterian or Pentecostal. The soil will work for whoever works the soil.

This is the way God is—He's an equal opportunity blesser. He shows no bias or favoritism based on the person. Instead, His favor is founded on faith.

Never worry over the size of the seed. It's the size of the harvest that is important. After all, the Word asks,

"Who despises the day of small things?" (Zechariah 4:10).

A seed certainly doesn't look anything like what it is going to become. I think back to the small group who gathered in the corner of a hotel ballroom in 1984 when we began our church. There were few in attendance who believed it would grow into the mighty ministry that touches thousands of lives today.

The Trust Factor

Let me reiterate that the giving of offerings into the Gospel has its foundation in the principle of sowing and reaping. Again, "A man reaps what he sows" (Galatians 6:7).

Most people demonstrate more faith in the soil of the earth than they do in God.

When you place the seed in the ground it requires trust. Most people demonstrate more faith in the soil of the earth than they do in God. They have total belief and trust that the earth will faithfully reproduce what is planted into it.

It is your seed faith giving that releases the ability of God financially in your life.

THE LINK TO CREATIVE POWER

When you take action by planting a seed, your faith level increases because you wouldn't take such a step unless you believed. And it is through faith that God links us to His creative power on earth—to seedtime and harvest.

Because of our experience in planting a garden, we know how to reap a natural harvest. But we are talking about what transpires when God gets involved.

However, the blessings we receive do not always have to be financial. The Lord pours His favor on us in many ways—through a strong marriage, wonderful children, caring friends, and good health. Yet these don't blossom automatically. Each requires a seed to be sown and nurtured.

IT'S NOT SELFISH

In the early days of our ministry a wealthy man invited Sue and me to a dinner party at his home. The guests included several prominent people from our community.

At the time we had a billboard in our city with these

words: "Jesus is Healing the Sick"—and the name of our church.

The host asked, "It seems to me that you are appealing for people to attend your church on a selfish basis."

Surprised, I responded, "Why do you say that?" and he referred to the billboard. I think I was being grilled!

He continued, "Do you want people just to come to church to be healed? Isn't that a bit selfish?"

I said, "No, it's intelligent."

If you stopped at the bakery to fill your tank, they'd think you had lost your marbles.

After all, why do you go to a gas station? To purchase gas. Does that make you a bad person?

If you stopped at the bakery to fill your tank, they'd think you had lost your marbles!

I explained to the host that when you are hurting, broke, sick, or need encouragement, what better place to go than to the house of God! It is where the Lord is always giving.

Giving Comes First

Jesus said, "Give, and it will be given to you. A good measure, pressed down, shaken together and running over, will be poured into your lap" (Luke 6:38).

The Lord didn't suggest, "When it is given to you—give."

Your act of giving is the first step. And when you do, what is returned to you is astounding. It is not only a *good* measure, but what is poured into our lap will be running over.

The act of sowing comes first; then the reaping. People may not even know why they are giving to you—but they will be God-inspired to do so.

I don't want God measuring my harvest with a teaspoon.

What the Lord said next is the part some don't like to read: "For with the measure you use, it will be measured to you" (verse 38).

Some people slip a $5 bill into the offering on Easter and Christmas and believe God for a harvest. This is not how it works.

I don't want my crop to be returned back to me in fives or tens, but in thousands! And I certainly don't want God measuring my harvest with a teaspoon.

"MANY MANSIONS"

Many believe that wanting material "stuff" is sinful. Well, if you think it is bad, perhaps you shouldn't go to heaven.

Jesus didn't say, "In my Father's house are many double-wides" or "many modular homes."

Rather, He said there are "many mansions" (John 14:2 KJV).

And since there won't be any railroads in heaven you can't live on the wrong side of the tracks!

More Productive to Give

The Son of God declared, "It is more blessed to give than to receive" (Act 20:35).

When we receive and don't give, that's a final act. But when we give, it is only the beginning. A multiplication process starts when you bring to God His tithe and your offerings. It keeps the multiplication process moving forward. But if you just receive, and stop there, it's over.

When a farmer pulls a thousand bushels of wheat out of the ground, he can measure his harvest. Yet if the same farmer were to plant the seed of a thousand bushels of wheat, he would have to find larger fields and prepare for the greatest harvest of his life.

The next time you bite into an apple, notice the number of seeds. Remember, the entire apple tree—roots, trunk, branches, leaves, and fruit—is the result of planting just one of those seeds. Imagine how many orchards that one apple can eventually produce.

When Jesus used the term "more blessed" regarding giving, He was letting us know, "It is more productive to give than to receive."

FIRST CLASS GIVERS

When I was growing up in Detroit we went on school field trips to museums that focused on the lives of great industrialists and inventors from Michigan—men such as Henry Ford, Thomas Edison, and Harvey Firestone, who greatly influenced our state.

These were original thinkers who created tens of thousands of jobs. And in the process they became world class philanthropists. In other words, they were first class givers.

Sadly, many of the foundations created by wealth have been taken over by individuals with extremely socialistic agendas. I believe if Henry Ford were alive today, he would put a stop to many of the grants given in his name.

THE ORIGINAL INTENT

Take a glance back in history and you'll find that the great universities—Harvard, Princeton, and Yale— were created for the training of ministers.

- Harvard was named after John Harvard, a young clergyman.
- Princeton was originally intended to produce Presbyterian preachers.
- Yale was also founded to educate clergymen.

Today the objectives of these institutions have drifted far from what their founding fathers envisioned.

He Gave it Away

Historically, immigrants are four times as likely to become millionaires in America than those who were born here. Many are of the opinion this is because these new citizens used creativity, initiative, and determination to succeed in their adopted land.

> ***What many are unaware of is that Carnegie was a lifelong tither.***

Andrew Carnegie is a prime example. He was born in Scotland, but came to Pennsylvania and made millions in the steel business. In his day, he was the richest man in the world.

What many are unaware of is that Carnegie was a

lifelong tither. And when he sold his steel business, he gave his entire fortune away—using most of the money to build over 3,000 libraries in the United States—plus many in other countries.

IT STARTED WITH $1.50

Carnegie wasn't the only wealthy man who was a tither. Oil magnate John D. Rockefeller stated, "I never would have been able to tithe the first million dollars I ever made if I had not tithed my first salary, which was $1.50 per week."

> ***"The more we give away, the more we have left."***

In the words of philanthropist John Templeton, "The more we give away the more we have left."

A 90 PERCENT GIVER

J. C. Penny—his middle name was actually "Cash"—was also faithful with his "tenth" to the Lord. Starting with one small department store in Wyoming, he built an empire that still has over 1,000 stores in 49 states.

As he grew financially, he realized he needed less to

live on. So he set a personal goal to give 20 percent to the Lord—then 30 percent. By the time J. C. Penny died, he was giving 90 percent to the church and living on the remainder. He was a walking example of a man who could not outgive God.

Some would say that Penny was wealthy so he could afford to give. I believe that because of his giving he became wealthy. Since he presented his tithe and offerings to the church, he gave God a *reason* to make him wealthy.

Great givers have a *motivation* for giving. And the more they give the more they want to. It becomes a driving force in their lives.

THE ANSWER FOR OUR PLANET

Today, with the social and cultural revolutions that have reordered our world, I am totally convinced that the only safe philanthropy is planting into the Gospel.

Without question, the best thing that can be done for our planet would be to see as many people commit their lives to Christ as possible—instead of blowing up airliners and bombing buildings.

In addition, a person living by God's principles will become a producer, not a drain on society. Such individuals work hard, pay their taxes, and abide by the laws of the land.

So the most effective use of our resources is to sow into the Gospel of the Lord Jesus Christ. I'm not saying that we have to give to just *any* church—because many are not propagating the Gospel. They have turned into "do-gooder" organizations that are secular instead of spiritual.

MAKE IT COUNT

Jesus asked, "When the Son of Man comes, will he find faith on the earth?" (Luke 18:8).

If we were all fulfilling the mission of wining people to Christ, think what this world would be.

> ***My heart aches when I hear of churches who hold pet fairs and serve popcorn and soda for communion.***

Joblessness would evaporate, tax receipts would skyrocket, crime would plummet, and most of the problems on our planet would disappear.

My heart aches when I hear of churches who hold pet fairs, and serve popcorn and soda for communion. It is astounding what goes on in the name of Christ.

We are to give, but to do so wisely.

Dreams and Aspirations

When you present your financial resources to the Lord, you are actually giving of yourself—your time, your education, your training, your labor, your ability.

The reason this is important is that through giving your dreams, goals, and aspirations are being multiplied.

Unfortunately, many are believing for a harvest that they have no right to claim. They are not tithing. They are not giving. They are not faithful. And as a result they are not blessed.

God pours out His abundance on people who live by His Word.

The Greatest Seed

Salvation began with the Holy Spirit of God planting a seed into a virgin's womb. An angel told Joseph, "Do not be afraid to take Mary home as your wife, because what is conceived in her is from the Holy Spirit. She will give birth to a son, and you are to give him the name Jesus, because he will save his people from their sins" (Matthew 1: 20-21).

As you study the life of Christ, you discover that He too became a seed.

Before Jesus was arrested, put on trial, and placed on a cross, He made this statement: "I tell you the truth, unless a kernel of wheat falls to the ground and dies, it remains only a single seed. But if it dies, it produces many seeds" (John 12:24).

In a parallel to Christ's death, burial, and resurrection, the seed has to die before it returns to life.

In a parallel to Christ's death, burial, and resurrection, the seed has to die before it returns to life.

God is a giver—because He gave His only begotten Son for our salvation. Christ is a giver—because He gave His life on the cross as a ransom for our sin.

As believers, giving should be our way of life.

THE 80-10-10 LIFE

Today I am praying that you will start walking on God's road of abundance. It begins with work—to produce the financial resources you need to begin this exciting journey.

Next, tell God you are committed to returning His tithe—10 percent of all that flows through your hands.

Then have the self-discipline to save and invest the next 10 percent so your wealth will grow.

Finally, by faith, start sowing your seed into the kingdom through offerings—over and above your tithe. This is where your financial life will be put on fast-forward.

If you make an unbreakable covenant with God to live the 80-10-10 life, I guarantee you will receive blessing, abundance, and the favor He has promised.

Don't waste one more minute. Start today!

FOR A COMPLETE LIST OF MEDIA RESOURCES
BY THE AUTHOR, CONTACT:

DR. GENE LINGERFELT
OVERCOMING FAITH CHRISTIAN CENTER
6900 US HWY 287
ARLINGTON, TEXAS 76001

PHONE: 817-561-3400
INTERNET: www.overcomingfaith.com